COOL, CALM, CONFIDENT YOU

COMPLETE HYPNOTHERAPY PROGRAM FOR CONFIDENCE - INCLUDES 3 HRS OF AUDIO HYPNOSIS DOWNLOADS

RICK SMITH - HPD DHYP

ricksmith hypnosis .com

The Copyright Bit...

This edition Copyright © 2018 by Rick Smith

All rights reserved.

No part of this book may be reproduced in any form or by any electronic or mechanical means, including information storage and retrieval systems, without written permission from the author, except for the use of brief quotations in a book review.

The Legal Bit...

I am a Certified Clinical Hypnotherapist. I am not a doctor or licensed medical practitioner, and I do not offer medical advice or diagnosis.

You're free to use hypnosis as you see fit, however if you have any doubts concerning it's efficacy in your case, you should seek guidance from a qualified medical practitioner.

Please do not play hypnosis recordings whilst driving or operating machinery.

Headphones or earbuds are recommended for privacy and effectiveness, when playing the hypnosis recordings.

CONTENTS

About the Author	v
1. Welcome to the Program	1
2. How This Works	9
3. The 'Cool, Calm, Confident You' Approach	19
4. Using The Recordings	25
SECTION 1 - HYPNOSIS TRAINING AND CONDITIONING	33
5. Why You Need This Training	34
6. Set-Up and Preparation	37
7. Stage One, Simple Induction and Emerge	45
8. Stage Two: Calibration - A Day At The Beach	52
9. The Training Transcripts	58
10. A Brief History of Hypnosis	72
SECTION 2 - COOL, CALM, CONFIDENT YOU	79
11. Cool, Calm, Confident You	80
12. Getting the Recordings	83
13. Session 1 - Value Yourself	88
14. Session 2 - Confident Control	92
15. Session 3 - Presentation & Performance Confidence	96
16. The Transcripts	99
17. Program Debrief	132
18. Other Rick Smith Programs & Books	134
Afterword	145

ABOUT THE AUTHOR

Rick Smith graduated as a Certified Clinical Hypnotherapist in London in 2006, and holds the NCH Hypnotherapist Practitioner Diploma from the Surrey Institute of Clinical Hypnotherapy.

His online practice, ricksmithhypnosis.com offers a variety of audio hypnosis programs covering areas such as Anxiety, Confidence, Workplace Stress, Procrastination, Weight Loss, and Health & Fitness.

Rick's first Amazon book, *How to Master Self-Hypnosis in a*

Weekend, has been a consistent bestseller since it's publication in 2013.

Other Rick Smith Hypnosis Books & Programs in this series are available from Amazon or as audiobook versions from www.ricksmithhypnosis.com

- Crush Anxiety Now
- Do It Now - Crush Procrastination
- The Determination Diet
- Active Energy Now - Exercise Motivation
- Sleep Fast, Sleep Deep, Sleep Now
- Crush Stress Now
- Master Self-Hypnosis in a Weekend
- The Motivation Code
- An Ocean of Calm - Ultimate Tranquility
- Breaking The Ice - Social Anxiety & Shyness
- Sugar Free - Crush Your Sugar Addiction
- Stop Hating Your Job - Banish Workplace Stress
- Own The Stage - Presentation & Performance Confidence

Why not join me on Facebook...

https://www.facebook.com/ricksmithhypnosis/

facebook.com/ricksmithhypnosis

1
WELCOME TO THE PROGRAM

Is your lack of confidence stopping you from living the life you want??

- MAYBE YOU'RE STRUGGLING with social situations? Wanting to start new friendships, but wary of putting yourself out there.

- Perhaps you want to be more confident in your work life? You've seen how more assertive people progress and succeed, and you'd like to be able to do that for yourself.

- Or are you facing presentation or performance anxiety? You have a great story to tell, but you're held back, anxious about the things that could go wrong, and ignoring the - more likely - outcome that everything goes right?

You're not alone.

Many people suffer all their lives, and never take action. Their philosophy? If you never try, you'll never fail.

But if you never take a risk, you'll never feel the elation of a well-earned reward.

Something in your past has shaped your view of who you are, how others see you, and what you can actually do. Listen: it's in the past, and quite likely incorrect. Whatever happened, or whatever was said, your subconscious mind absorbed it, and established it as part of your belief system.

But it's really not part of who you are; you weren't born that way. You've *learned* to be shy, or lack faith in yourself in certain situations, and this has been holding you back, possibly for years.

The good news...

Your mind is programmed to keep you safe, and it's setting you a low bar. Perhaps you avoid anything which has the remotest risk of failure or embarrassment? You see danger signals when there usually isn't any danger.

What we show to others is how they form their opinions of us. If the signals we're sending out aren't getting us what we'd like to be getting back, it plays right into the hands of your safety-first subconscious mind, which then steers you away from similar situations in the future.

The good news is this: just as you learned to believe this artificial, incorrect information about yourself, you can learn a different way to behave, one that uses no more effort or intelligence, but which will have a more positive, beneficial outcome.

Make the changes...

In **Cool, Calm, Confident You,** you'll be re-discovering strengths you've unwittingly suppressed or buried, and learning how to put them together and make them work for you, in your new, confident, persona.

It's rather like upgrading your software with a version which makes better use of your resources, and delivers you a more satisfactory outcome than the previous version.

These hypnosis tools will empower you to modify your emotional responses and remove your unnecessary obstructions to living a fuller, more confident life.

Once you've understood the rewards, you'll be highly motivated to learn and practice the methods of obtaining them.

This book is an extended version of my original audio download program. It includes:

- An overview of this program, the hypnosis methods we'll be using, and full instructions to prepare you for hypnosis
- My two-part thirty-minute hypnosis training and conditioning audio program, to get you used to going in and out of hypnosis, smoothly and easily. If you're already used to hypnosis, or you've completed any of my other programs, you can skim through this section, or skip it altogether.
- Three targeted hypnotherapy sessions to directly address the key components of your confidence, totalling around two hours of professionally recorded hypnotherapy.

You can download or stream the recorded sessions, free for life, by following the simple instructions in Chapter 4.

Never play these recordings whilst driving or operating any kind of machinery. Please be responsible (I know you are).

How I Know This Works

There's a lot of snake-oil out there in the hypnosis industry, so why should you trust me?

Well, you already know that I'm certified (that's the big-shot letters after my name) so I'm ethically bound to provide my best professional efforts to my clients.

But if you need more: Here's a screenshot from my online store, which sells these programs in audio download format. As you can see, 42% of my sales are to returning customers (as of October 2018).

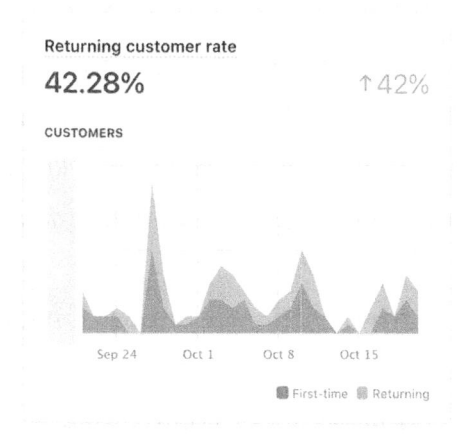

Returning customer rate
42.28% ↑ 42%
CUSTOMERS

Sep 24   Oct 1   Oct 8   Oct 15

■ First-time ■ Returning

So I guess it works!

Recordings vs. Face-to-Face Hypnotherapy

So, how does recorded hypnotherapy compare to a visit to the hypnotherapist's office?

Does this way work the same?

Well, it's not exactly the same, primarily because some conventional - *analytical* - hypnotherapy techniques require two-way communication between therapist and client, which is clearly impractical for us.

However, that doesn't mean it's less effective. Far from it!

Imagine this;

- You book an appointment with your nearest hypnotherapist, probably a few days in advance.
- For days you worry about the visit; *will it work, will I like the therapist, can I afford the cost, can I get time off?*
- The day arrives, and you're already anxious about the journey, apprehensive of meeting a stranger, unhappy about the weather, and concerned about your work or family situation.
- You struggle downtown, with all the inconvenience and cost, and finally arrive, unsettled and stressed, for your session.
- You now put yourself in the hands of a complete

stranger, and spend the first half of the session wondering if it's working.
- By the time you're relaxed, it's over, and you have to battle your way back home, maybe more than a hundred pounds or dollars lighter.
- Once you get home, you try to replicate what the therapist taught you, but half of it's just a distant memory.

You may give up completely. Your problem wasn't solved.

The Alternative;

- You decide to try hypnotherapy to boost your Confidence.
- You buy, beg, borrow or steal a copy of *Cool, Calm, Confident You* which will never be more than seven pounds / ten dollars.
- You find a quiet, comfortable space at home, put on your headphones, and listen to the sessions, which I've specifically created and adapted to work effectively in a *one-way* environment.
- You practice your new skills straight away, and repeat your hypnosis sessions whenever necessary, anytime, anywhere.

Now, how's that *not* going to work better?

Of course, there are many complex conditions which can't readily be adapted for audio hypnotherapy, and which really do benefit from the live clinical experience. That's why I don't publish programs about depression, addiction (except sugar addiction!) or grief.

Pretty much everything else works just fine!

2
HOW THIS WORKS

How Does It Work?

FORMS OF HYPNOSIS have been a regular feature of ancient civilisations, some of whose rituals survive to this day. Shaman, Faith Healers, Cults and Religions have used and continue to use forms of hypnosis with their followers. Chanting, music and singing, sermonising, meditation, and even the use of psychoactive substances, natural and unnatural, are used to induce transient states in their followers.

Hypnotherapy is the practice of inducing this *trance state* in an individual (that's the *hypno* part) which suppresses your conscious critical faculty and enables carefully-crafted, congruent verbal communication to pass directly through the usual filters, to communicate with parts of the mind that are usually closed off to direct access - the subconscious - where habits and behaviours are stored and operated.

Everyday things like walking, talking, and eating are down there, as well as more complex skills that we acquire through our lives, like driving or tightrope walking!

Your subconscious mind is responsible for your automatic responses; how you act or behave in a specific situation. Such responses are learned over time, and sometimes, if some distorted information has been fed in - usually quite early in your life - your response to certain situations may be off-centre, causing you problems.

That's where the *therapy* part comes in. Whilst you're suspended in that open-minded, accepting state, the hypnotherapist will use his skills to change or adapt replace your habits and behaviour, over-writing your old, troublesome beliefs and responses with more appropriate new ones.

When hypnotised, you're able to accept these new 'machine instructions' unquestioningly, because the skilled therapist will demonstrate to you that your new way of doing things is more beneficial, and serves you better, than your old way.

As this is the primary directive of your automated subconscious – to protect you and ensure you thrive – it's readily accepted, and with application and repetition, your new habits are embedded for good.

The Stages

Hypnotherapy has several stages. Each one segues directly into the next, ensuring that the whole process is smooth and relaxed, with no bumps in the road.

1. Preamble

In the first stage, you're encouraged to find a comfortable position, and simply listen to an introduction. This preamble is intended to start the ball rolling, and focus you on the subject or issue you're going to be working on in hypnosis. Although this is not strictly part of the trance, it's a very important component of the process, and should ever be skipped.

2. Induction

At the appropriate moment, you'll be encouraged to close your eyes and begin the induction process. In this phase, the therapist uses a range of relaxation, visualisation, and imagination techniques to guide your descent to an adequate depth of trance for the work to begin.

There are many different forms of induction, some fast, some not so much.

In my courses, I start off using a specially modified medium-length and highly effective induction – the *Dave Elman Induction* – which is one of the most popular amongst experienced hypnotherapists.

In subsequent sessions, I introduce shorter, more rapid inductions, once you, the client, are conditioned to going easily into hypnosis.

3. The 'Work'

Once you are sufficiently deep in the hypnotic state, however that comes to you, the work can begin. Depending on the issue, there are a wide variety of 'therapeutic' approaches which can be used.

Here are just a few:

- *Visualisation*
- *Sensory Simulation*
- *Age Regression*
- *Time Compression*
- *Metaphor*
- *Coaching Techniques*
- *Breathing Techniques*
- *Re-Framing*
- *Triggers and Anchors*
- *Self-Hypnosis*
- *Pattern Interruption*
- *Modified Self-Talk*
- *Ego Strengthening*

For my programs, given the obvious limitation of tailoring the approach for each individual client, I have concentrated on using the optimum combination of techniques for these one-way recorded sessions.

We won't be delving into the dark corners of your life (if you have any) looking for eureka moments. You won't be beating your chest or clucking like a chicken either, I'm afraid.

You'll just be focusing on accepting that you need to make a change, and then making it happen, in the most appropriate, beneficial way.

4. The Emerge

Once the work is completed, you'll be gently guided back to a full waking state. You may remember everything, or you may remember nothing at all. As we said in the beginning, everyone experiences it differently, and I'm pleased to report there seems to be no correlation between 'reported' depth of trance and the effectiveness of the program.

5. The Debrief

After the Emerge phase, you'll be invited to review what happened, and the changes you have made. In many cases, I'll be setting you some homework, to practice what you've learned, and help to drive your new habits deeper so they stay strong and permanent.

This real-life work is equally as important as the hypnosis, because regular practice of your new way of doing things reinforces your new synapses, those connections in your brain which carry the messages between its different parts.

This is the science of neuroplasticity, the ability of the brain to rewire itself when required to do so. It works.

The State

So, now you understand how it works, how does it feel? And how will you know when you reach it?

It's practically impossible to describe the sensations of hypnosis to someone who's never experienced it, for two reasons.

- Firstly, because there are many, many different states, often unique to an individual. How someone relaxes and *lets go* is always coloured by their life, situation and environment. Everyone accepts hypnosis in their own unique way.
- Secondly, the state of hypnosis defies words, at least words of sufficient eloquence to describe it adequately. Can you describe how you felt in the last minute before you fell asleep last night?

You'll be familiar with that *in-between state between awake and asleep,* when your mind wanders and you start to dream, sometimes in short flashes, in between the little naps that drift in and out. So if you know how that feels, you'll be close to understanding how hypnosis feels – like hovering in that state, still aware, but otherwise detached from your physical environment.

But you won't have the words to describe it adequately, so there's no need to try.

Just accept it, and enjoy the experience.

Using The Scripts and Recordings

Each of the hypnosis scripts is printed long-hand in this book. If you want to, you can read and record the scripts yourself. Around one-in-fifty of my clients and readers appear to opt for that.

If you want a quicker fix - maybe you prefer not to listen to your own voice - I've recorded them for you, with my (professional hypnotherapist's) voice, and you can download or stream these recordings free of charge for life. The access instructions are in the Chapter 4.

It's easy, I promise.

I recommend you use your smartphone, mp3 player, or tablet computer as the quickest and most convenient method. You can carry the recordings with you, so you can use them anywhere, anytime. I've included instructions about how to do this on Apple and Android devices, and I'm sure if you're a Windows, Sony, or Blackberry user, you'll be able to adapt these instructions for your own device.

If you encounter any issues, please e-mail me at rick@ricksmithhypnosis.com and I'll fix it for you. A few of my Amazon reviewers have complained that they couldn't access the scripts in the past, and punished me with one or two stars. These issues are invariably down to a user's own settings, so if you mail me you'll get a quick solution, and I'll avoid any more negative reviews!

If you don't use a portable device, you can play the recordings from your PC or Mac. Somewhere in the world, somebody's probably listening to them on a cassette player or even an 8-track. Let me know if it's you!

You can download or stream the scripts by clicking the link at the beginning of the next chapter. You'll receive an immediate e-mail with your access details.

The System

Repetition is a key strategy with hypnosis of any kind, and you'll discover lots of opportunities to drop into trance and practice your skills.

Everything you need to know, and everything you need to do, is laid out in sequence. All you need to succeed is to follow the system.

If you enjoy the program and you find it useful, please take a moment to post a review on Amazon. When my first hypnosis audio/book - *How to Master Self-Hypnosis in a Weekend* - was published in 2013, there were maybe twenty books on the subject. Now there are hundreds, and most of them are disappointing, so if you find this book worthwhile, please help others to discover it by reviewing it. Thanks.

Now, just relax and enjoy the ride.

3
THE 'COOL, CALM, CONFIDENT YOU' APPROACH

FIRST OF ALL, I'd like to welcome you to this program, and congratulate you on taking a big step towards achieving your confidence goals, whatever they may be.

Maybe you're struggling with social situations, wanting to form new friendships, but wary of putting yourself out there.

Perhaps you want to be more confident in your work life: you've seen how more assertive people progress and succeed, and you'd like to be able to do that for yourself.

Or are you facing presentation or performance anxiety: you have a good story to tell but you're held back, anxious about the things that could go wrong, and ignoring the more likely outcome that everything goes right.

You're not alone; Many people suffer all their lives, and never acknowledge that they need help to get on top of the problem.

At the root of most confidence issues is an event, a series of events, or a longer-term issue in your past which has shaped your view of who you are, how others see you, and what you can actually do. Although whatever caused you to doubt yourself is real, it's in the past, and quite likely incorrect. Whatever happened, or whatever was said, your subconscious mind absorbed it, and in the absence of a balancing influence, such as praise for your efforts and achievements, has reinforced it over time and established it as part of your belief system.

But it's really not part of who you are; you weren't born that way. You've learned, by some perverse or distorted means, to be shy, or lack faith in yourself in certain situations, and this has been holding you back, possibly for years.

The good news is that, just as you learned to believe this artificial, incorrect information about yourself, and have behaved according to that model ever since, you can learn a different way to behave, one that uses no more effort or intelligence on your part, but which will have a more positive, beneficial outcome.

Your mind is programmed to keep you safe, and by

enabling a low threshold of safety, that is to say that you avoid anything which has the remotest risk of failure or embarrassment, you've consistently allowed your mind to signal danger when there usually isn't any. It's an overgrown version of the old saying "Once bitten, Twice Shy", and it manifests itself as a lack of confidence. If you never try, you'll never fail, and if you never take a risk, you'll never feel the elation of a well-earned reward.

So, you have all the necessary resources, mental and physical, to do this. Our hypnosis together will be all about finding the strengths you've unwittingly suppressed or buried, and teaching you how to put them together and make them work for you, in your new, confident, persona.

Sounds easy, doesn't it, but we both know there'll be some effort involved. Luckily, you'll be doing all the work inside your head, whilst relaxing to the sound of my voice, guiding you at all times. In hypnotic trance, your subconscious mind, the one that thinks it' keeping you safe, when it's actually holding you back, is open to accept new suggestions and behaviours which will make more sense than the current ones. It's rather like upgrading your software with a version which makes better use of your resources, and gives you a more satisfactory outcome than the previous version.

Before we embark on this journey, there's something else I'd like to mention.

If I ask you to think about confident people that you know, and I mean people you've interacted with in the past, maybe people you work with now, or even friends and family, do you always believe that they're naturally confident, and that it takes no effort on their part?

Well, in some cases you'd be right, but in most cases you'd be surprised at the processes that these people go through to achieve that outward display of confidence.

A lot of them will, essentially, be faking it, because they've made a bargain with themselves that they must do what they need to do in order to achieve the outcome they seek. That's about motivation, the eye on the prize. If it doesn't come easily, act like it does. It doesn't really matter if it's real or fake, so long as you get the desired outcome.

But what does matter is how you feel about it, before, during, and afterwards.

If you want to get more marriage proposals, you have to go on more dates. And if you show up with a smile on your face and a spring in your step, no-one will know if you're feeling it or faking it!

What we show to others is how they form their opinions

of us, and what they give us back informs our self-image. If the signals we're sending out aren't getting us what we'd like to be getting back, it plays right into the hands of your safety-first subconscious mind, which then steers you away from similar situations in the future.

But with the application of a few simple tools, which we'll be exploring in our hypnosis session shortly, you can control that process by following a logical sequence.

At first, it might feel like you're acting, but that's the route we're going to take to get you used to feeling how a confident person feels when they need to be at their best. Once you've understood the rewards, you'll be highly motivated to learn the methods of obtaining them.

When those two systems work together, that's where the magic happens.

Training and Conditioning

As with all my courses and programs, this one will work many times better and faster if you're comfortable going in and out of trance. If you've tried hypnosis or hypnotherapy in the past, and feel that it worked for you, you should be fine.

If this is your first time, I recommend you complete my

two short Training and Conditioning recordings before you set to work on your confidence.

Hypnosis is progressive, and the more often you do it, the faster, smoother, and deeper it becomes. By conditioning yourself with the training sessions, you'll find the therapeutic value of the main recordings will be many times more effective.

The Training and Conditioning recordings come free in your download package, and the transcripts are printed long-hand in Section 1.

When you're ready to begin, make yourself comfortable and make sure you won't be disturbed. Draw the shades, eliminate any distracting noises, and prepare yourself to be hypnotised.

Each of the recordings has a short introduction, or preamble, following which you'll begin the hypnosis.

4
USING THE RECORDINGS

IN THIS CHAPTER, we're going to look at two important practical aspects of this hypnosis program;

- How to access and use the recorded sessions, using your computer, smartphone or tablet,
- Preparing and setting up your ideal hypnosis environment.

The Hard Way - Record It for Yourself

In the next section, the scripts are printed long-hand. You can read and record them yourself, using your smartphone's Voice Memo or Voice Recorder function (or any other recording device), and then play them back as many times as you need.

If you're using your smartphone as the recording device, the easiest way to record your own voice is to use the microphone attached to your hands-free headphones. This avoids you having to hold the phone and gives you easier access to the controls. You'll be able to pause and re-start the recording as needed.

However, listening to your own voice is not ideal, and you probably don't have experience in reciting hypnosis scripts, which rely for their effectiveness on certain voice techniques.

So, although this is a perfectly practical way to work with the scripts in this book, I seriously recommend you use my pre-recorded versions as explained below. You'll get a better result and it will be much quicker to get started.

The Easy Way - Using My Recordings

All the scripts I used to create these recordings are included in the book. The Training Scripts are at the end of Section 1, and the Main Scripts are in Section 2.

Many clients buy my hypnotherapy programs as audio-books from my website. The recordings you'll be accessing through this book are the same high-quality audio downloads, and you're free to download or stream them whenever you like.

How to Get the Recordings

The recordings are securely stored on Amazon Web Services (AWS) so that they can be played or downloaded 24/7. I chose AWS to host my recordings (more than 200, at last count) because of their platform's reliability and easy access for you, my client, on any device.

By the way, they're not paying me to say that!

If you experience any difficulties in accessing these recorded sessions, please e-mail me at **helpdesk@ricksmithhypnosis.com** and I will solve it for you.

My hypnosis recordings have been downloaded more than 30,000 times, and I receive one or two help-desk emails in an average week. I've simplified the access process so you should have no issues, but please get in touch if you do.

So, let's get you organised right now:

When you click on this link (or type it into your browser if you're reading the print version) it will open up a little form on your screen. Please enter your first name and your email address and submit the form.

That's all you need to do.

http://tiny.cc/amzconf

You should receive an email from **rick@ricksmithhypnosis.com** within a minute or two, containing your access information. Please keep this email safe, so you can access the sessions anytime.

It's not unknown for this first e-mail to go into your junk folder, so please check there first if you don't receive it within three minutes of registering.

In the email you receive, you will have two options. You can use either or both:

On Your Computer

The individual audio files are MP3's, the same as a song you might download from iTunes or Google Play.

Because the tracks are longer (30-60 minutes each), and there are several tracks in each program, they've been compressed and packaged into what's called a 'Zip' file, to make them easier and faster to deliver by download.

If you opt to download the .zip file, you will get the complete program (it may take a few minutes) on your computer's hard drive. From there, you click on it and it will open and unpack the individual recordings as MP3's.

Once you can see each of the individual tracks, you can

simply play each one by clicking on it, or you can transfer the tracks (just like music) to your phone or tablet, using whatever method you would usually use for songs. If you're struggling with this, ask a nearby teenager to help you!

Alternately, use the links for streaming or downloading each individual mp3 recording. Using your computer's web browser, by copying or typing the link, the audio file will open (it may start to play). I recommend you pause the audio, then right-click on it, selecting 'Save Audio As'. This should open a file saving dialogue box, and you can download and save the mp3 file in your music library.

Once you've done that, you can open your music player (such as iTunes) and find the track in the alphabetic list of all your stored music tracks. The artist name is Rick Smith.

If you download it to your 'Downloads' or 'Desktop', you can play the recordings direct, or open iTunes or your preferred music player, and import the file.

You can play it from there, or alternately you might decide to create a new Playlist (perhaps call it 'Hypnosis Sessions') and drag the track into it. Then you'll easily be able to find it, and when you sync to your phone or tablet next time, make sure you add the playlist and you'll be able to find it easily on your device, which is where you really need it to be.

On Your Phone or Tablet

Downloading the whole program's *zip* file to your phone or tablet isn't an option for most people, because these devices don't usually have a file system to open and store the tracks.

Apple users are at a particular disadvantage here. I'm all Apple over here, and I haven't yet found an elegant way to do this on any of my devices.

So instead, you can access the individual sessions and play (stream) them live, wherever you have Wi-Fi or data available.

Your *welcome and access email* will show you where to find the recordings, and it's one simple click to start, pause, or stop them at any time.

If you decide to go this way, you can be up and running on your portable device within three minutes of clicking or typing the link below, and you can always go back and download the whole program when you're near your computer.

This means you can access the recordings from anywhere you have data access. Each recorded session is typically

30-40MB (equivalent to 6 - 8 mp3 songs), so please be careful if you have a limited data plan with your phone carrier. Wi-fi, particularly at home, is often free or unlimited, so that's the best and most economical way to access the recordings.

Whenever you use your portable device for playing scripts - which you'll be doing a lot throughout this course - please use headphones or earbuds for privacy. This also helps to block out external noises, which can be a distraction during your hypnosis sessions.

All set? Good. Here's a reminder of the link that will get you rapid access to the recordings for this program.

http://tiny.cc/amzconf

And if you hit any snags, email me here:

helpdesk@ricksmithhypnosis.com

I'm not a corporation with a call centre. There's just me here, with a couple of dogs and the odd visitor. If you email during European daytime/evening, I'll fix it for you within an hour or two. If you're outside my time zone (for example North America, or Australia) it might take a little longer!

Now, go and get the recordings, and once you have them, we'll talk about the ideal set-up.

SECTION 1 - HYPNOSIS TRAINING AND CONDITIONING

5

WHY YOU NEED THIS TRAINING

IF YOU'RE TRYING hypnosis for the first time, you'll benefit from some training and conditioning before we set to work on your Confidence in Part Two.

If you're confident with hypnosis, and ready to get stuck in to the serious stuff, you can skip straight to Chapter 11 and start the main program.

However, even if you don't want to read this section, I'd still encourage you to play the two training recordings at least once, to refresh your skills and get you in the mood, so to speak.

You can complete the whole training program in an hour or so, and doing so will greatly enhance the effects of the main recordings in Part 2.

If you've never tried hypnosis before, please do this training program. The recordings in Part 2 are *Intermediate* level and are designed to work best with clients who are well-conditioned in advance. These *Beginner* scripts will get you ready.

This initial training program contains two fifteen-minute recordings:

1. **Training Session 1 - Basic Induction.** This first session will allow you to experience hypnosis and trance, maybe for the first time in your life. You can repeat it as often as you like, and the more you use it, the more comfortable and confident you'll become with the whole hypnosis process.

You don't have to do anything except relax and enjoy the experience.

2. **Training Session 2 - Visualisation and Calibration.** In the second script, you'll explore your own capabilities whilst in hypnosis. You'll discover your *modality*; how you see, hear, and feel whilst hypnotised.

Once again, you may repeat this session several times, and your depth of trance and imagination skills will improve each time.

By the time you've completed these two sessions, you'll be ready to move on and get serious about your confidence.

6
SET-UP AND PREPARATION

IN ORDER TO give yourself the best opportunity for success with hypnosis, you need to pay attention to your immediate environment. The more ideal you can make the set-up, the more relaxed you will become, and the fewer distractions are likely to occur.

Most of these instructions are simple common sense, but you'd be surprised at how many people ignore the obvious!

Privacy

In the early stages, whilst you're learning the basics, you need to shut yourself away somewhere private, and make sure you won't be disturbed. There's nothing to be gained by having someone else listening in or involving themselves in the process.

If you live alone, it's simple. If you have family or flatmates, it's up to you if you decide to tell them what you are planning to do. In my view it's always better to come clean, because when you finally shut yourself away to practice, you really need to eliminate any concerns that you're doing something covert or sneaky, or that someone might think it's silly if they accidentally discover what you're doing.

You don't want to be trying to descend into trance whilst keeping one ear open for approaching footsteps!

If you're going to eliminate distraction - which is essential for this process to work - you must *control your environment*.

Tranquillity

Silence in your hypnosis environment is ideal, although it may be difficult to achieve, especially if you live in a city. Nevertheless you should strive to establish the quietest possible space for your hypnosis.

Close the doors and windows and switch your phone to 'Flight Mode' so that it won't ring or vibrate. Anything which disrupts your concentration whilst you're doing the exercise might take you back to the beginning. Once you're well-practiced at this, you'll be able to deal with external sounds as part of the trance, but at the beginning, until you've mastered the process, you need to eliminate as much external disturbance as possible.

You'll probably be using headphones, which will block most external noise, depending on the kind you use.

I regularly used headphones for my clients and a headset microphone for myself in my London practice, which was just 2000ft below the flight path for Heathrow airport!

Your Personal Comforts

As you've understood, achieving the hypnotic state will always go better if you eliminate distractions, which includes physical distractions.

- Wear clothing that doesn't pinch or constrict. You may want to remove your shoes, belt, and watch.
- Visit the the bathroom before you start. A call of nature half-way though your session is difficult to ignore, and it will probably mean starting the session all over again.
- Make sure the room temperature is comfortable; not too cool and not too warm.

Where to Sit

If you visit a professional hypnotherapist, you'll rarely see a couch or flat-bed in their office, and there's a good reason for this.

As you can imagine, taking people into a state of deep relaxation can run the risk of them falling asleep, especially if they arrive tired for the session. If you're lying down, the risk is increased, because this is most people's natural sleeping position.

If a client nods off during hypnosis, the session is essentially over, because your hearing shuts down as soon as you're asleep and nothing goes in, apart from the noise of a fire alarm or a wake-up call!

Falling asleep during hypnosis is not uncommon, and it's completely harmless. Once asleep, the hypnosis is muted, and anything that happens whilst you're asleep won't be effective.

Within the scope of the hypnosis exercises you'll do in this course, you can be sure that you'll eventually wake up 'out of trance', so no harm done. But you could waste time and effort, which is why you should try to avoid lying horizontally if possible.

Of course, if you have no alternative comfortable location, the hypnosis itself will work fine on a couch or bed, but you need to be aware of the heightened risk of snoozing through the best bit!

The ideal situation is a comfortable chair: even a recliner if you have access to one. Try to have your legs uncrossed and your feet flat on the floor. You should make sure your head and neck are supported with a cushion.

Where to put your hands is really related to how you would normally sit to relax. I've found that most clients like it if I give them cushion to put on their lap and then they can rest their hands on it.

A competent professional hypnotist can work on clients

in almost any position, and if you've ever seen a good stage hypnotist, you'll have seen subjects put into trance whilst standing up. This is genuine, but it takes special training and immense confidence to master.

For your purposes, you should try to get as close to the picture as you can manage. As long as you're comfortable, and you don't need to tense any muscles to maintain your position, this will work just fine.

Stimulants

Stimulants can be an issue, so you should avoid them. Coffee in particular can inhibit relaxation, so it's best to avoid drinking it before you're going to work on your hypnosis skills.

Later, once you've mastered dropping in and out of hypnosis at will, it won't make much difference. But in the early stages, you're trying to eliminate every possible obstacle to you being able to enjoy the relaxation state that leads to hypnotic trance.

If you're a smoker, especially if you're using hypnosis in order to help you quit, I recommend that you thoroughly cleanse your breath and hands before you start. In hypnosis, your senses can sometimes sharpen unexpectedly, and the smell of tobacco could become intrusive once all other distractions are suppressed or eliminated, which could trigger a craving.

Of course – and this probably goes without saying – alcohol and drugs don't go well with hypnosis. It's virtually impossible to hypnotise a drunk, and although I did once manage to put a hardcore stoner into a deep trance - after many attempts - the work we tried to do once he was hypnotised was completely ineffective!

Other drugs are mainly stimulants, and it's pointless to try.

Light and Dark

Given the choice I would always prefer to practice hypnosis in a dimmer room. You may have to open and close your eyes a number of times during the process, and if the room is bright this can tend to kick you out of trance more quickly.

How dark is really a matter of personal preference. During the day you should close your shades or blinds so that there is still natural light in the room, but no bright light source. If you're practicing in the evening, a side-lamp is better than a bright ceiling lamp. Try to make sure it's out of your line of sight.

That's just about it for your environment. Most of these

tips are obvious, but they all combine to create the most conducive situation for you to succeed at hypnosis, so try to consider each one in terms of its practicality for you.

So, you've got your recording ready, and you're seated and relaxed in a comfortable, private environment.

You're all set, so let's get on with the first exercise.

7
STAGE ONE, SIMPLE INDUCTION AND EMERGE

What You'll Be Doing

IN THIS FIRST EXERCISE, we're going to use a standard hypnosis *induction* to start to get you used to how hypnosis works.

If you've visited a professional hypnotherapist in the past, it's possible that the induction part of your session may have been quite a prolonged affair. Many therapists use a technique called 'progressive relaxation' to take you gradually into a light trance, and then slowly deepen the state over anything up to an hour. This works fine for most people, but it takes a long time.

Rapid Induction

A famous American hypnotherapist, Dave Elman, having observed the apparent need to repeat this long-winded conditioning exercise, developed a very successful alternative which accelerates the induction process. I have been using this *Elman Induction* with clients for more than a decade, and found that it works well every time.

This induction compresses the repetitive conditioning into a series of brief *mini-inductions* which start to induce hypnosis through relaxation, then momentarily wake up the subject, before repeating the process again and again. The technique ensures that each time the subject opens his or her eyes, then drops back towards the trance state, they go deeper.

The result is a nicely hypnotised subject in a matter of a few short minutes. This is the technique we will be using in our first Training Exercise.

What To Expect

You won't be expected to make any earth-shattering discoveries at first, however each time you repeat this exercise you'll find that you'll become more confident and inquisitive.

Whilst you're in this light hypnotic state, you may find that you can begin to visualise scenes, places, or events. Alternately you may experience feelings or emotions, which can often become quite intense.

How you experience hypnosis will depend on you as an individual, whether you're principally visual, auditory or kinaesthetic by nature, or maybe a combination of any or all of these.

After an appropriate period of quiet time, my voice will gently emerge you from your hypnotic state, until you're wide awake, back in the room, and feeling great.

During Your Trance

Hypnosis is completely safe, and you will never lose your ability to wake yourself up if you feel uncomfortable with what's going on. The likelihood is that you'll wonder about this, sometime during your experience, but you'll feel so good that you won't feel the need to try to wake yourself up. I invite you to test this for yourself once you've gone through the induction stage.

There are three accepted stages of hypnotic trance which most professional hypnotherapists use. For the purpose of this explanation, we'll call them *light, medium, and deep*. In professional practice, the *deep* state is often used for treating really serious psychological conditions, as well as medical and dental anaesthesia.

It's unlikely (though possible) that you'll ever reach a state of deep (*comatose*) hypnotic trance using recorded hypnosis. Even if you do, the techniques contained in these scripts will work in exactly the same way, to emerge you back to your full waking state when it's time.

In this first exercise, we'll be targeting the *light* state. In this state, most people remain fully aware of where they are and what's going on around them, but they choose to 'switch off' that consciousness and 'go inside' to explore their own internal thoughts, images, and feelings.

You may achieve this light state on your very first attempt. You may even recognise it when it happens, or you may perhaps feel that nothing has changed, and you're just relaxing in a chair with your eyes closed. It doesn't matter, because each time you go into hypnosis you'll go deeper than the last time, and you'll discover new sensations and experiences which will encourage you to go further.

Remember, it's a *conditioning* process, and the more often you do it, the better you'll become.

When you emerge from your first hypnotic experience,

we're going to conduct a little de-brief, so that you can reflect on how you got on.

So, make yourself comfortable, put on your headphones, and when you're ready, **start the recording**.

∽

De-Brief

Welcome back!

How was that for you? Why don't you stretch now, I'm sure you feel like it. You completed the exercise really well.

Now, just take moment to reflect on what happened. You might remember everything, or you might remember nothing at all. It may have seemed like a really short time, or alternately you might feel like you've been gone for ages. I can tell you that the whole exercise took less than fifteen minutes.

When you're completely ready, you're going to start the recording again and repeat the experience, but this time you will easily go much deeper into hypnosis, and each time that you do this you will be able to go deeper still.

Right now, I suggest you get up and walk around for a few

minutes, maybe have a cup of tea or a glass of water. Remember, no coffee and preferably no smoking! Then when you're ready to try it again, come back and make yourself comfortable.

De-Briefing Yourself

After the first time you try the exercise, there may be things that you noticed which you can change in order to make it easier next time. Just run through the check-list below, and make any adjustments before the next repetition.

- *Temperature*: was I too warm or too cold?
- *Comfort*: how was my seating position, the position of my hands, and so on?
- *Volume*: was the recording too loud, too soft?
- *Brightness*: do I need to lighten or darken the room?
- *External sounds*: was I distracted? Do I need to stop anything, close any windows, and so on?

These are small things, but any one of them can detract from the overall experience, so it's really worth taking a little time to get everything right, so that there are no obstacles to you achieving that wonderful depth of relaxation which hypnosis offers.

You can go on repeating this exercise as many times as you like. You'll be the best judge how well it's working for you, and you'll notice the progressive conditioning as you try it again, and again.

Although my voice is guiding you, the actual hypnosis is coming from you. You're allowing it to happen, and it is happening. That's the essence of hypnosis.

You should not think about moving on until you're entirely comfortable with this first exercise. Many people report that the second time they do it, it's much more effective than the first, and this is the conditioning effect we discussed earlier. Just keep repeating the recording as many times as you like. There's no such thing as too much practice!

Next, in Stage Two, we're going to use the skills that you've developed in Stage One to train you to use the hypnotic state to do new things.

8

STAGE TWO: CALIBRATION - A DAY AT THE BEACH

Exercise Two

NOW WE'LL USE another recorded script which starts off with a similar induction to the one we used before.

Once you're in trance, you will be given a *trigger word*, which is 'BEACH' and your task is to experience everything associated with being at a beach.

The idea is to *calibrate* you so that you'll be able to tell if you're predominately *visual*, *auditory* or *kinaesthetic*, whether you see, hear, or feel more strongly in hypnosis. How you experience the beach will determine what we call your *modality*, and this will help you to anticipate and understand how to harness hypnosis' benefits in the future.

You'll be using your powerful imagination, which allows you to roam freely in hypnosis. If you're primarily visual, you may be able to generate a clear image of the beach scene and to be able to describe it, either during the trance or afterwards.

Maybe you'll be primarily auditory, in which case you may hear the sounds of the waves, or children playing in the sand.

Alternately - if you are primarily kinaesthetic - you might feel the breeze on your face, or smell the salty air.

It's entirely possible that you may experience more than one of these modalities, which is great, and it's also possible you'll form a multi-sensual impression, neither one thing or another, but which will work just as well.

This sessions called "Hypnosis Training Session 2" and you can download or stream it just the same as the first one.

Parts of the script may be familiar to you, which should help you to drop into hypnosis very easily. However, some of the parts are shortened because you simply don't need all the deepening techniques now that you've become proficient.

Again, if you insist on recording your own scripts, this one's printed long-hand in the next chapter.

Once you have the recording ready, make yourself comfortable and quickly run through the checklist below:

- Switch your phone to Flight Mode if you've downloaded the recording. If you're going to stream it (over wi-fi) select the setting which leaves the wi-fi on but turns calls and notifications off.
- Make sure you won't be disturbed for around fifteen minutes.
- Visit the bathroom if you need to.
- Take a few moments to acclimatise yourself to any sounds that you may hear during the exercise, and explain to yourself that these will not disturb you.

When you're completely ready, **start the recording** and enjoy the trance!

∼

De-Brief

If you followed the preparation instructions and stuck to the recorded script, you should be quite amazed by now, at your own ability to enter hypnosis and what you can do whilst you're there.

The Beach scene often evokes powerful imagery or sensations in people who try this exercise, and I'm sure you experienced something like that too. If, for some reason, it wasn't as vivid or literal as you'd hoped, don't worry. Just play it again, even two or three times, and the effect will increase as you get more proficient at exercising your powerful imagination.

You'll remember from the introduction that this was called a *calibration* exercise, and the idea was to try to discover your modality, that is to say are you predominately visual, auditory or kinaesthetic. Your experience at the beach should have given you a good idea of this.

Did you see the colours? Were they bright or dull? Did you see movement, or was it like a post-card? If any of these statements are true for you, make a mental note of the answers so that you can build your future visualisations around your strengths.

Maybe you didn't see much, but you heard the sounds. Could you hear the waves, the seagulls, the people talking and kids playing? Maybe you heard a more elaborate sound-track, like a beach bar or a restaurant with music. Again, try to recall what you were hearing and make a mental note of how vivid it was, how complex and/or realistic the experience.

Or maybe you mainly felt *things*, like breeze, smell, or texture? Maybe what you experienced was an 'impression' of the beach, enough to convince you that you were there, even though you couldn't see or hear very much? That's called kinaesthetic.

You should now be able to assess and decide your dominant *modality*. If you can't do it yet, I suggest you run the recording again, now that you know what to expect, and spend some more time at the beach!

You'll have accomplished this part of the mission when you're able to say to yourself: *"I am predominately visual/auditory/kinaesthetic."*

Remember, you don't have to have only ONE modality, but you should try to identify your dominant one, because that's the way that you'll approach your exercises when you start doing more interesting things with your hypnosis.

By now you should be dropping easily into trance, and you should be totally confident in your own ability. You can completely let go and enjoy the experience, and you should also have convinced yourself that each time you do it, you go deeper.

Once you feel comfortable with this process, you'll be ready to move on to the main event.

See you there.

THE TRAINING TRANSCRIPTS

Session 1 Transcript

*W*HEN YOU'RE *ready to enter hypnosis, take a long deep breath and hold it for a few seconds. As you exhale this breath, allow your eyes to close and let go of the surface tension in your body. Just let your body relax as much as possible right now.*

Now, place your awareness on your eye muscles and relax the muscles around your eyes to the point they just won't work. When you're sure they're so relaxed that as long as you hold on to this relaxation they just won't work, hold on to that relaxation and test them to make sure <u>THEY WON'T WORK.</u>

Now, this relaxation you have in your eyes is the same quality of relaxation that I want you to have throughout your whole body. So, just let this quality of relaxation flow through your whole body from the top of your head to the tips of your toes.

Now, we can deepen this relaxation much more. In a moment, I'm going to have you open and close your eyes. When you close your eyes, that's your signal to let this feeling of relaxation become 10 times deeper. All you have to do is want it to happen and you can make it happen very easily. OK, now, open your eyes... now close your eyes and feel that relaxation flowing through your entire body, taking you much deeper. Use your wonderful imagination and imagine your whole body is covered and wrapped in a warm blanket of relaxation.

Now, we can deepen this relaxation much more. In a moment, I'm going to have you open and close your eyes one more time. Again, when you close your eyes, double the relaxation you now have. Make it become twice as deep. OK, now once more, open your eyes ... close your eyes and double your relaxation... Good. Let every muscle in your body become so relaxed that as long as you hold on to this quality of relaxation, every muscle of your body will not work.

In a moment, I'm going to have you open and close your eyes one more time. Again, when you close your eyes, double the relaxation you now have. Make it become twice as deep. OK, now once more open your eyes... close your eyes and double your relaxation... Good. Let every muscle in your body become so relaxed that as long as you hold on to this quality of relaxation every muscle of your body will not work.

Now, that's complete physical relaxation. I want you to know that there are two ways a person can relax. You can physically relax and you can relax mentally. You already proved that you can relax physically, now let me show you how to relax mentally.

In a moment, I'll ask you to begin slowly counting backwards, in your mind, from 100. Now, here's the secret to mental relaxation; with each number you say, you'll double your mental relaxation. With each number you say, let your mind become twice as relaxed. Now, if you do this, by the time you reach the number 97, or maybe even sooner, your mind will have become so relaxed, you will actually have relaxed all the rest of the numbers (that would have come after 97) right out of your mind. There just won't be any more numbers. Those numbers will leave, if you will them away. Now, start with the idea that you will make that happen and you can easily dispel them from your mind.

Now, in your mind say the first number, 100 and double your mental relaxation. Now the next number..... Good.... Now double that mental relaxation. Let those numbers already start to fade. Next number.....Double your mental relaxation. Start to make those numbers leave. They'll go if you will them away. Now, they'll be gone. Dispel them. Banish them. Make it happen, you can do it, Push them out. Make it happen! THEY ARE ALL GONE

That's fine. The mind is relaxed and the body's relaxed. Just let yourself relax much more with every single breath. And I do want your body to relax just a little bit more so let me help you do that. This time I will count from 5 down to 1. With every number I say, let your mind and body relax together like a team so that by the time I reach the count of one, mentally and physically you easily let yourself relax much more. All right?

5-deeper--that's good—4 - 3 --that's fine-2 – deeper down and --------------- 1.

That's great, doing fine. I'd like you now to see if you would allow yourself, to let yourself, to go to your very basement of your ability to relax. And you know there is no real basement of a person's ability because we've never found a basement, only on every particular instant in time your basement can be many, many times deeper. And I'll help you to get there.

I want you to imagine that there are three more levels to take you to your basement of your relaxation.--levels -A, B, and C. To get to-level A,- you--simply- double the relaxation that you have now. To get to level B, you must double the relaxation you have in level A. And finally to get to your basement, you must at least double what you have in level B. To help you with this, I want you to use that powerful imagination of yours. And I want you to imagine that you're standing at the top of your own private escalator, like they have at the shopping centre only this is your own private escalator.

I am going to count to 3 - and at the count of 3, you'll step onto your escalator that will be taking you from where you are now down to level A, double the relaxation that you have now. When you get there, you'll let yourself know by simply raising one finger gently. Here we go-1-2-3. Step on to the escalator and go down, deeper down, doubling that relaxation which feels so good. When you reach the next level, step off your escalator and relax. Good, wonderful.

Now in a moment we're going to go from level A to level B. To get to level B, you simply have to double the relaxation that you're allowing in level A. Just let it grow twice as deep. All right. Imagine yourself at the top of your next escalator. Here we go, 1-2-3 and step on... Let it take you all the way down where you will have doubled your relaxation. Now, if you're following these instructions, you may find it difficult to move your finger, but that doesn't matter at all. But try anyway. Just take all the time you need to get to level B--- and when you arrive at the bottom of that escalator, step off and relax. Good.

Now there's one more level that I'd like you to go to: Level C -- the very basement of your ability to relax. Once more, find yourself at the top of that escalator. At the count of three, step on and it will take you all the way down to level C -- the very *basement of your ability to relax today. Here we go: -1-2-3. - deeper-deeper-letting go-deeper-deeper-deeper-to the very basement of your relaxation-drifting down-much more relaxed. OK. That's fine. Way down. Now just let yourself stay there for a moment and notice at this level every breath you exhale just easily helps you relax even more. Every breath takes you deeper and deeper relaxed.*

Now as you relax, drifting deeper with every word I speak, the first thing I would like you to know is how much I appreciate and admire you for the decision you have made to try hypnosis for yourself and to explore the wonderful benefits that it can add to your life.

Now you have those physical signs that allow you to know that you have moved from one conscious state to another in a calm and confident way. In this calm and confident state you can offer yourself generous portions of self confidence... large helpings of self-esteem, breathing out self-doubt as you relax even deeper and continue to enjoy the journey towards your goal.

Now you're going to take a short period of silence, relaxed in this beautiful hypnotic state, and experience whatever comes to you. See what you see, hear what you hear, feel what you feel, and simply let the waves of physical and mental relaxation wash over you.

(Pause)

You've done great.

In a moment, I'm going to count from ONE up to THREE. At the count of three your eyes are going to open, become fully alert, totally refreshed. Any cobwebs that you might have had, any sleepiness of mind is going to dissolve and disappear, and you're going to feel bright eyed and full of energy. You'll be fully alert and wonderful and marvellous in every way.

ONE, slowly easily and gently feel yourself coming back up to your full awareness.

At the count of TWO you're still relaxed and calm but notice that your eyes under your eyelids feel as if they're clearing, kind of like they're being bathed in a sparkling cool mountain stream, you feel GREAT.

On the next count those eyes are going to open, totally alert, fully refreshed, just feeling excited, wonderful, in every way, and every time you go into hypnosis you can let yourself go deeper than the time before because you know that just feels good.

All right, get ready, and on the count of THREE open those eyes and notice how good you feel.

Session 2

Self-Calibration Transcript

When you are ready to enter trance once more, take a long deep breath and hold it for a few seconds. Now exhale this breath and allow your eyes to close and let go of the surface tension in your body. Just let your body relax as much as possible as you've done so many times before.

Now, place your awareness on your eye muscles and relax the muscles around your eyes to the point they just won't work. When you're sure they're so relaxed that as long as you hold on to this relaxation they just won't work, hold on to that relaxation and test them to make sure THEY JUST WON'T WORK.

Now, this relaxation you have in your eyes is the same quality of relaxation that I want you to have throughout your whole body. So, just let this quality of relaxation flow through your whole body from the top of your head to the tips of your toes.

Now, you know that can deepen this relaxation much more. In a moment, you're going to open and close your eyes. When you close your eyes, that's your signal to let this feeling of relaxation become 10 times deeper. You want it to happen and you have proved that you can make it happen very easily. OK, now, open your eyes... and close your eyes and feel that relaxation flowing through your entire body, taking you much deeper. Use your wonderful imagination and imagine your whole body is covered and wrapped in a warm blanket of relaxation.

Now, you can deepen this relaxation much more. In a moment, you're going to open and close your eyes one more time. Again, when you close your eyes, double the relaxation you now have. Make it become twice as deep. OK, now once more, open your eyes ... and close your eyes and double your relaxation. That feels SO good. Let every muscle in your body become so relaxed that as long as you hold on to this quality of relaxation, every muscle of your body will not work.

In a moment, you're going to open and close your eyes one more time. Again, when you close your eyes, double the relaxation you have now. Make it become twice as deep, as you did so many times before. OK, now once more open your eyes... and close your eyes and double your relaxation... excellent. Let every muscle in your body become so relaxed that as long as you hold on to this quality of relaxation every muscle in your body just will not work.

Now that you're totally physically relaxed. You are going to easily relax mentally. You already proved that you can relax physically, now you know exactly how to relax mentally.

In a moment, you'll to begin slowly counting backwards, in your mind, from 100. And with each number you say, you will double your mental relaxation. With each number that you say, let your mind become twice as relaxed. Start to count, and by the time you reach the number 97, or maybe even sooner, your mind will have become so relaxed, you will actually have relaxed all the rest of the numbers right out of your mind. There just won't be any more numbers. Those numbers will leave, if you make them go away. You have proved that you can make that happen and you can easily dispel them from your mind. Now, start counting backwards from 100 and make those numbers disappear. Each number that you say will double your mental relaxation. Start to make those numbers leave. They'll go if you will them away. Now, they'll be gone. Dispel them. Banish them. Make it happen, you can do it, Push them out. Make it happen! Good, THEY ARE ALL GONE

Well done. Your mind is relaxed and your body's relaxed. Just let yourself relax much more with every single breath. And I do want your body to relax just a little bit more so let me help you do that. This time I will count from 5 down to 1. With every number I say, let your mind and body relax together like a team so that by the time I reach the count of one, mentally and physically you easily let yourself relax much more. All right?

5-deeper--that's good—4 - 3 --that's fine-2 – deeper down and - --------------- 1.

That's great, doing fine. Now that you are so relaxed, you're going to go even deeper, and you already know how to do this. Imagine the escalators which will carry you down towards the basement of your ability to relax even deeper.

You know that there are three more levels to take you to your basement of your relaxation.--levels -A, B, and C. As you go deeper to each level double the relaxation that you have now. Use that powerful imagination of yours so that you're standing at the top of your private escalator and when I count to 3, Step on to your escalator and it will be taking you from where you are now down to level A, double the relaxation that you have now. When you get there, you'll signal by simply raising one finger gently. Here we go-1-2-3 and down you go, deeper into relaxation. Good, wonderful. (Pause)

Now in a moment we're going to go from level A to level B just like before. To get to level B, you simply have to double the relaxation that you're allowing in level A. Just let it grow twice as deep. All right. Imagine yourself at the top of your next escalator. Here we go, 1-2-3. And step on. Let it take you all the way down where you will have doubled your relaxation. Just take all the time you need to get to level B--- [WAIT]--Good.

Now there's one more level that you know you can go to: level C--the very basement of your ability to relax. Once more, find yourself at the top of that escalator. At the count of three, , it'll take you all the way down to level C -- the very basement of your ability to relax. Here we go-1-2-3. Step on... -deeper-deeper-letting go-deeper-deeper-deeper-to the very basement of your relaxation-drifting down-much more relaxed. OK. That's fine. Way down.

Now just let yourself stay there for a moment and notice at this level every breath you exhale just easily helps you relax even more. Every breath takes you deeper and deeper relaxed.

And now you know how amazing and easy it is to get to this deep place of relaxation, and you are welcome to remain in this beautiful place as long as you want and to come here again any time that you like, because you KNOW how to relax your body and mind completely and let go so you relax so completely.

Now you have those physical signs that allow you to know that you have moved from one conscious state to another in a calm and confident way. In this calm and confident state you can offer yourself generous portions of self confidence... large helpings of self-esteem, breathing out self-doubt as you relax even deeper and continue to enjoy the journey towards your goal.

Take a few moments to appreciate the peace and tranquillity in this deep place that you have brought yourself to. (Short Pause)

Now, imagine you are at the Beach and it's a lovely day.

(Pause) See what you see, hear what you hear, feel what you feel. Take a moment to experience how it is, there at the beach. Allow your powerful, wonderful imagination to transport you there and be at the beach, however that is for you.

If you can see where you are, say "I can see it", or if you can hear the sounds around you say "I can hear it" and if you can feel the warmth, the breeze, and the texture of the sand, say "I can feel it". Go on, just say out loud what is happening to you, and your imagination of this wonderful beach will grow stronger. Allow yourself to feel how good it is to be at the beach, how relaxed and comfortable you are and just rest there for a few moments, taking it all in.

(Pause)

And now you know new things, and that knowledge empowers you. You know about this beach, and how wonderfully relaxing it is to be here, and you know that you can return here any time you choose because you have proven the power of your wonderful imagination and your amazing ability to bring yourself to this wonderful state of deep relaxation any time that you choose, so easily. And I want you now to remember what happened to you at the beach today, what you saw and what you heard and what you felt, so that you can remind yourself later about this amazing beach and your clever ability to come here again. Just relax quietly for a few moments and take it all in.

(Silence for two minutes)

Now it's time for you to leave the beach for now, so let your imagination gently fade.

You've done great. PAUSE. In a moment I'm going to count from ONE up to THREE. At the count of three your eyes are going to open, become fully alert, totally refreshed. Any cobwebs that you might have had, any sleepiness of mind is going to dissolve and disappear, and you're going to feel bright eyed and full of energy.

You'll be fully alert and wonderful and marvellous in every way. ONE, slowly easily and gently feel yourself coming back up to your full awareness.

At the count of TWO you're still relaxed and calm but notice that your eyes under your eyelids feel as if they're clearing, kind of like they're being bathed in a sparkling cool mountain stream, you feel GREAT.

On the next count those eyes are going to open, totally alert, fully refreshed, just feeling excited, wonderful, in every way, and every time you go into hypnosis you can let yourself go deeper than the time before because you know that just feels good. All right, get ready, and on the count of THREE open those eyes and notice how good you feel.

∼

10
A BRIEF HISTORY OF HYPNOSIS

IF YOU'RE interested in how hypnosis and hypnotherapy evolved to where we are today, this short section might interest you.

If you'd rather get stuck in to the real stuff, you can skip this section; it won't make any difference to your experience with hypnosis.

What most people understand about hypnosis is largely grounded in two areas. On a personal level, you may have tried it, or know someone else who has tried it. Alternately, you'll have seen it on TV or at a theatre show.

The fundamental technique of hypnosis is 'congruent communication', particularly verbal communication. But the myriad of studies suggests that the process is much more complicated and sophisticated than that.

The urban legend that we only use 10% or 20% of our brains is an oversimplification, but it's entirely possible that we are only 20% competent in the use of *all* our brain faculties. This, of course, is the essence of training of any kind.

Hypnosis is a major part of the armoury of Witch Doctors and Shaman, as well as Faith Healers and Con Artists, who've been around since the dawn of time. It could be argued that the radicalisation of vulnerable young people by fundamentalist zealots owes a lot to hypnosis.

Some schools of thought believe that part of natural evolution is the understanding of the conscious ability to tap into the subconscious rhythmic operation of the brain and the body as a whole.

It seems likely that all the faculties required to enter a hypnotic state exist within a person's own mind, and that the role of the outside force such as the shaman or hypnotist is to guide the subject into accessing resources which are normally hidden, and to implant the skills to enable them to do it repetitively.

In the 18th century, a physician called Franz Mesmer identified the hypnotic state, and coined the term "animal magnetism", believing that it was an intangible fluid blessed with healing powers that was able to exert mutual influence between the Universe, the Earth and Animal Bodies, especially humans. He equated this fluid state as being magnetic in nature, and conducted many experiments using magnetism to demonstrate a natural or enhanced behaviour in humans and animals. In his most famous case, Mesmer treated a blind pianist and apparently restored her sight.

Unfortunately, given the political and religious environment of the day, Mesmer was labelled a fraud, and died in relative obscurity in Switzerland in 1815. However he left behind the term *mesmerised*.

Two notable British pioneers of hypnosis took the science forward in the 1800's. James Esdaile was a surgeon who used hypnotic anaesthesia successfully in hundreds of surgical operations, and in modern hypnosis the deepest state of trance is often still referred to as the *Esdaile State*.

James Braid, also a physician, was particularly struck by an exhibition of mesmerism by the French expert Lafontaine, and took up intensive research thereafter. During this time there was some confusion as to whether hypnosis was a state of sleep, and Braid's induction methods were based on eye fatigue. Braid's research has only become relevant and interesting in the 20th and 21st centuries, and he did not achieve much of a profile in his day.

After Braid, recorded research moved to France, and great strides were made in the use of hypnosis as a receptacle for suggestion techniques, and the language structures of *suggestion* started to develop. Sigmund Freud experimented with hypnosis for some time but eventually discarded it, probably because it did not offer him many advantages in his psychoanalytical work.

Fast-forward to the 1950s, and the era of Dave Elman. Elman was relatively low-key, but was widely regarded and respected in the medical and psychological communities in the USA. Elman may be credited with having taken away a lot of the mystique surrounding hypnosis.

Hypnotists of the day appear to have been somewhat anal in enhancing and dramatising the science and the therapies involved in it. There was also a great deal of fear around at the time, and the spectre of *electric shock therapy* in the mental health system frightened many people away from what they saw as *mental medicine*.

Elman dramatically simplified the definitions of hypnosis and also the techniques used to induce it. These days, confident hypnotists still employ the Elman induction, because it enables them to take most patients into a appropriate state of trance in between five and ten minutes, rather than the thirty minute inductions favoured by the more traditional branch of science.

I use the Elman induction (a lot) in my own hypnotherapy sessions, and it works well on almost everyone, saving a lot of time in the preamble stage and enabling more of the session to be devoted to actually solving the clients' issues.

Post flower-power, a new branch of hypnosis and psycho-analysis emerged, most notably under the leadership of Richard Bandler and John Grinder. The original concepts of *Neuro Linguistic Programming (NLP)* were laid out for the world in their breakthrough book "Frogs to Kings". Richard Bandler has gone on to have a colourful career but remains at the pinnacle of the NLP movement. His description of NLP as *waking hypnosis* may be viewed as something of a paradox, since modern science confirms that all hypnosis is conducted in a waking state.

Nevertheless, NLP aids the comprehension of language; how spoken conversation can be formatted to cut through someone's critical function and exert positive influence on the subconscious and instinctive part of the personality.

If you want to see a consummate NLP practitioner in action, I recommend watching one of Bill Clinton's big speeches, which can be found on YouTube. If you watch it, try to identify the small snippets of patterned language which may sound occasionally incongruous, but are carefully crafted to induce approval, compliance, or a favourable opinion from the audience.

Probably the best-known hypnotist in the UK, and subsequently in America, is Paul McKenna. McKenna makes hypnosis look easy, but he is without doubt an outstanding exponent of the science. McKenna is not just able to hypnotise people, but he has the sixth sense which allows him to quickly empathise with the subject, and thinking on his feet, use rapid techniques to effect a change. He's rich because he's good at this. I've spent some time training with both Richard Bandler and Paul McKenna, separately and together, and the experience was scintillating.

Many people credit Dave Elman with the quotation *"all hypnosis is self hypnosis."* The role of the hypnotist can be as a trainer. If you ever learned to ski, you can understand how it's possible to train a new skill into someone of any age from a zero start, usually in a matter of hours.

Hypnosis is a similar process: you have all the resources to enable you to do this, but you need a guide and a trainer to explain the system by which you access them and make them work.

SECTION 2 - COOL, CALM, CONFIDENT YOU

11
COOL, CALM, CONFIDENT YOU

Welcome (again) to the program.

In this Three Part hypnosis series, you'll be guided and trained to assume new habits and behaviours, which will be more useful than the ones that are currently holding you back.

In the first session, we'll examine and remove some of the common obstacles to confidence. You'll learn to separate who you are from how you feel, and replace the way your feelings cause you to act with more appropriate responses. You have all the necessary resources: our objective is to over-write unhelpful beliefs and behaviour with habits more suited to the confident person you've now decided to become.

In the second session, we'll examine your part in your own life, and you'll discover the qualities you already possess that make you unique and special. In this module, you'll come to understand that you have all you need to control what happens, before, during, and after any confidence-testing situation. Millions of confident people do things this way, and you can model their methods, and succeed for yourself.

In the third session, we'll be dealing with Presentation or Performance Confidence. Whether you're delivering your first business presentation, or you still get nervous after years on the theatre stage, this is a well-proven hypnosis approach which has been shown to work effectively. If your lifestyle or career depends on a confident approach to public speaking or performance, this session will equip you with the right tools to achieve that every time.

If this is your first experience with hypnosis, or you haven't done it for a long time, please use my two Training Recordings which came with your download. They won't take long, but they will condition you to be comfortable going in and out of trance, and then the Confidence sessions will work better and faster.

When you're ready to begin, make yourself comfortable and make sure you won't be disturbed. Draw the shades, eliminate any distracting noises, and prepare yourself to be hypnotised. Each of the three recordings has a short introduction, or pre-amble, following which you'll begin the hypnosis.

Let's begin.

12
GETTING THE RECORDINGS

Getting Your Recordings

IF YOU ALREADY HAVE THE recordings, you can jump straight to **Session 1**.

If you came straight here and missed out Section One (Training and Conditioning), here's a reminder of how to access and use the recorded hypnosis sessions for this program.

I've simplified the access process so you should have no issues, but please get in touch if you do.

Let's get you organised right now:

When you click on this link (or type it into your browser if you're reading the print version) it will open up a little form on your screen. Please enter your first name and your email address and submit the form. That's all you need to do.

http://tiny.cc/amzconf

You'll then receive an email from **rick@ricksmithhypnosis.com** within a minute or two, containing your access information. Please keep this email safe, so you can access the sessions anytime.

It's not unknown for this first e-mail to go into your junk folder, so please check there first if you don't receive it within three minutes of registering.

In the email you receive, you will have several options.

Quick Start

Just click on the Session link (1,2, or 3) in the email and it will start to play (provided you're online) on any device.

Download or Play on your Computer

The individual audio files are MP3's, the same as a song you might download from iTunes or Google Play.

Because the tracks are longer (30-45 minutes each), and there are several tracks in each program, they've been compressed and packaged into what's called a 'Zip' file, to make them easier and faster to deliver by download.

If you opt to download the .zip file, you will get the complete program (it may take a few minutes) on your computer's hard drive. From there, you click on it and it will open and unpack the individual recordings as MP3's.

Once you can see each of the individual tracks, you can simply play each one by clicking on it, or you can transfer the tracks (just like music) to your phone or tablet, using whatever method you would usually use for songs. If you're struggling with this, ask a nearby teenager to help you!

Alternately use the links for streaming or downloading each individual mp3 recording. Using your computer's web browser, by copying or typing the link, the audio file will open (it may start to play). I recommend you pause the audio, then right-click on it, selecting 'Save Audio As'.

This should open a file saving dialogue box, and you can download and save the mp3 file in your music library. Once you've done that, you can open your music player (such as iTunes) and find the track in the alphabetic list of all your stored music tracks. The artist name is Rick Smith.

If you download it to your 'Downloads' or 'Desktop', you can then open iTunes or your preferred music player, and import the file from there.

You can play it from there, or alternately you might decide to create a new Playlist (perhaps call it 'Hypnosis Sessions') and drag the track into it. Then you'll easily be able to find it, and when you sync to your phone or tablet next time, make sure you add the playlist and you'll be able to find it easily on your device, which is where you really need it to be.

On Your Phone or Tablet

Downloading the whole program's *zip* file to your phone or tablet isn't an option for most people, because these devices don't usually have a file system to open and store the tracks.

Apple users are at a particular disadvantage here. I'm all Apple over here, and I haven't yet found an elegant way to do this on any of my devices.

So, instead you can access the individual sessions and play (stream) them live, wherever you have Wi-Fi or data available.

Your *welcome and access email* will show you where to find the recordings, and it's one simple click to start, pause, or stop them at any time.

If you decide to go this way, you can be up and running on your portable device within three minutes of clicking or typing the link below, and you can always go back and download the whole program when you're near your computer.

This means you can access recordings from anywhere you have data access. Each recorded session is typically 30-40MB (equivalent to 6 - 8 mp3 songs), so please be careful if you have a limited data plan with your phone carrier. Wi-fi, particularly at home, is often free or unlimited, so that's the best and most economical way to access the recordings.

Whenever you use your portable device for playing scripts - which you'll be doing a lot throughout this course - please use headphones or earbuds for privacy. This also helps to block out external noises, which can be a distraction during your hypnosis sessions.

All set? Good. Here's the link again that will get you rapid access to the recordings for this program.

http://tiny.cc/amzconf

And if you hit any snags, email me here:

helpdesk@ricksmithhypnosis.com

SESSION 1 - VALUE YOURSELF

THIS INTRODUCTION IS ALSO INCLUDED in the audio download for Session 1.

Introduction to Session 1

Now that you're comfortably seated and ready to begin, it might be useful for you to understand and appreciate the nature of confidence.

As we work together, it helps for you to separate the feelings that you associate with confidence, in this case a deficit, which causes you to take avoiding actions and you now believe this is for your own safety.

So, what is confidence?

Confidence is simply a feeling of security that you possess sufficient resources to manage yourself appropriately through unfamiliar or challenging situations. It's a normal state for a minority, and a challenge for most of us.

Confidence is derived from...

A sense of self-worth, a belief that you are equal to everyone else, that your personal defining qualities are clear to you and to them.

Confident action works best if you have a good understanding of others' expectations, and a well-established, appropriate set of boundaries.

Resulting in...

A calm, measured approach to tasks or situations, knowledge that you can perform as needed, and an outward communication of your confidence, which gives others confidence in you.

By committing to these hypnosis sessions, you will be committing to acquiring and embedding these useful attributes into your everyday life.

The first level of confidence I'd like you to now practice is to be confident in the hypnosis process itself, which is about to take place. We'll go in slowly in order to achieve a satisfactory level of working trance, so you can now allow yourself to relax completely, and simply listen to the sound of my voice.

PLAY THE SESSION 1 RECORDING NOW

Debrief

Welcome back! How as that for you? Why don't you have a stretch now, I'm sure you feel like one. You completed the exercise really well. Now just take moment to reflect on what happened. You might remember everything, or you might remember nothing at all. It may have seemed like a really short time, or alternately you might feel like you've been gone for ages. I can tell you that the whole exercise took less than fifteen minutes.

You may have experienced some strong feelings during the trance: that's intentional. You've learned already that your imagination is so powerful that it can cause feelings and emotions which are exactly the same, sometimes even more intense, than real-life feelings.

This is really useful in hypnosis because it allows you to sample how real things are going to feel, without having to actually take the risk of doing them. So you can test out the value of an experience in hypnosis, and then you know, as you do now, how good it feels to achieve difficult or challenging things, whereas before you might not even have tried them at all. You now know that it was your old, out of date safety mechanisms that were holding you back, and there's really nothing to be afraid of in everyday life.

Use this recording often. It's packed full of useful techniques that will build and multiply the more often you simulate them, and then practice them in real life.

In the next session, will be exploring and removing some of the irrational and limiting beliefs which may be obstructing you, and equipping you with a systematic process to prepare, execute, and review your approach to confidently approaching challenging situations, events, or relationships.

Thanks for attending this session, and I look forward to working with you again in the next one, whenever you're ready to begin.

∼

SESSION 2 - CONFIDENT CONTROL

T*HIS INTRODUCTION IS ALSO INCLUDED* in the audio download for Session 2.

Session 2 Introduction

Welcome back. I hope you've had a chance to practice with the new skills you learned in the first recording.

Maybe you feel like you've begun the journey, and now you're ready to reinforce your new behaviour and start to put it into practice.

This second recording can also be used in bed at night, as there is no emerge section or debrief at the end, so if you fall asleep afterwards, that's great.

Now, let's be honest; you didn't start this hypnosis course hoping you could be more confident whilst sitting on your couch, now did you? Of course not.

Increasing your confidence is all about freeing you from any artificial constraints or limitations you may have been putting on yourself, even excuses you've been using, to avoid entering situations which you think may be uncomfortable for you.

It doesn't mean you're suddenly going to launch yourself out into the world, accept every invitation you receive, and dazzle everyone you meet with your new levels of charm and charisma, though of course this is yours to do, if that's your desire.

No, this is about taking things at your own speed. You can practice your feelings of confidence and self-esteem in these hypnosis sessions, and the more often you do that, the more natural and familiar they will become.

These are your trainer wheels, and before you know it, you'll be balancing perfectly upright without them.

Let's briefly recap what you achieved in the first session.

First of all, you're special. There's probably no-one else around with the same mix of skills, experiences, and abilities as you. And don't forget, everything counts. Even things you've experienced that didn't go so well are important because of the lessons that you learned. But where an event or experience had maybe affected your confidence or self-esteem in the past, you now know that it was a safety mechanism that was being over-protective of you, and now you're older and wiser, you can leave things like that behind, because you have no further use for them

Secondly, you're equal. Your fundamental right to take a full part in the world around you is the same as everyone else's. You possess the same basic attributes and resources that everyone has, and you start each day from the same position, equal to everyone. Showing respect or deference is simply good manners, it doesn't make you any less equal. Neither is arrogance or superiority an admirable trait. Treat everyone equally, as you would like to be treated yourself. Your equality lives inside you, and you owe it to yourself to consider it in every action you take.

And thirdly, how good it feels to achieve things and put them behind you. Your mind is largely based on reward structures, which fire chemicals like dopamine and serotonin into your brain to reward you with good feelings when they're appropriate. By actively focusing on a positive outcome whenever you need a confidence boost, you'd be amazed at how calm, rational, and even dispassionate you can become in the face of challenges that might have blocked you in the past.

Always keep your eye on the prize.

So now you've absorbed and adopted the main behaviour patterns used by calm, confident people. You have the foundations on which you can now build something special, so when you're ready to explore the next part of your journey, simply prepare yourself to enter hypnosis once again. We'll be following a familiar path to enter the trance, so all you need to do is relax and listen to the sound of my voice.

PLAY THE SESSION 2 RECORDING NOW

Debrief

There's no debrief for this session, so it can be used at bed-time.

∼

SESSION 3 - PRESENTATION & PERFORMANCE CONFIDENCE

This introduction is also included in the audio download for Session 3.

Session 3 Introduction

Welcome back; In the first two sessions you learned some important secrets about self-worth and equality, and how to employ simple physical rituals to change the chemical balance in your body and the actions of your internal nervous system.

The objective was to implant a more appropriate set of responses, new habits that will become increasingly automatic as you practise them each day.

Everything that you previously thought was holding you

back is now rationalised. You know that – in reality - there's nothing to fear, so you can set aside your old safety-first response, and guide yourself forwards in every aspect of your life.

In this session, we're going to move to the ultimate test of confidence, and that is presenting or performing in front of an audience. Even if this isn't something you plan to do, the exercise will be equally useful to you.

Just before we start, there's something I'd like you to bring with you, that will help us to make the work we're doing many times more effective. Please concentrate for moment, go inside, and bring up an image, or just an impression or feeling, of an event, or more generally just the type of event that you'd like to be more confident in approaching. It would be useful for you to know where you are, why you're there, and who else is in the room. Let me give you a moment to do that.

PLAY THE SESSION 3 RECORDING NOW

Debrief

Welcome back, I hope you enjoyed that?

That trance took around 35 minutes, and you achieved a

lot in that time. You learned several new techniques which you'll now be using regularly, as confidence building is cumulative. These things work, for thousands of performers and presenters, and maybe you'll adapt what you've learned for your specific situation. However it works for you, the principles are solid; you can now control every aspect of your preparation and delivery, ensuring that you arrive on the day, fully rehearsed, and eager to nail it.

THE TRANSCRIPTS

Session 1 Transcript

Now, take a long deep breath and hold it for a few seconds. As you exhale this breath, allow your eyes to close and let go of the surface tension in your body. Just let your body relax as much as possible right now, as you've done so often before. We will take it slowly so you can go deeper than the last time.

Now, place your awareness on your eye muscles and relax the muscles around your eyes to the point they just won't work. When you're sure they're so relaxed that as long as you hold on to this relaxation they just won't work, hold on to that relaxation and test them to make sure THEY JUST WON'T WORK.

Now, this relaxation you have in your eyes is the same quality of relaxation that I want you to have throughout your whole body. So, just let this quality of relaxation flow through your whole body from the top of your head to the tips of your toes.

Just let that relaxation permeate and dissipate through all your muscles, all your joints, and feel the tension as it releases you from physical constraints,.

Just let your body go completely limp and lazy, and when you feel that you've relaxed as much as you can, go further, and let yourself explore all the different parts of your body to make sure you have fully relaxed them.

Your arms, loose and limp from your shoulders all the way down past your elbows, through your wrists and into your hands, releasing every microscopically tiny bit of tension or stress right down to the tips of your fingers, that's right.

Your legs, which work so hard every day, now completely relaxed and disengaged, just like your whole body now, quietly parked in this safe place until you need it again.

Now, that's complete physical relaxation. And you already know that there are two ways a person can relax. You can physically relax and you can relax mentally. You already proved that you can relax physically, now let me remind you how to relax mentally.

Allow your mind now to drift out and away from your body, because you won't need your body for a little while, so your mind is free to explore, free to go wherever you will it to take you.

And as you feel your mind drift outward and upwards, you're alert but relaxed and tranquil and you may begin to perceive white light all around you, as your mind clears of the trivial, practical things, and opens up to new information, and a more beneficial way of thinking and responding.

Just let your mind drift a little higher now, and when you find the equilibrium, the balance you seek, that comfortable place where you can simply be, ready to learn, and eager to progress, just rest there and refresh yourself for a moment.

<<Pause>>

The Work

As you now embark on this journey, we should take a moment mark your achievements, which have already begun with you taking the first steps. You have decided to make changes, and these changes you have decided to make will alter and enhance your life from this day forwards.

And the phrase 'this day forwards' is more important to you today than before, and more important to you than it is to other people, because on this day, the changes you make will be creating a new version of you; an upgraded version that replaces the previous version; the old you.

Some of the features of your previous version are redundant now. You don't need them any longer.

Some of the features of the old version of you were originally put there to keep you safe when you were younger and maybe more vulnerable.

But you're not vulnerable now; you're all grown up and stronger, and something that may have affected your confidence or self-esteem in the past probably wouldn't bother you in the slightest today.

So, this old, redundant safety feature has been removed from the new, upgraded version of you that you're getting ready to welcome today.

You don't need that old habit any more. You're good at making yourself feel safe and secure, because you have a great deal of experience from life itself, and you've successfully lived it so far.

In your imagination you may now form an impression of your old self, holding back, maybe anxious and shy; see what you see, hear what you hear, and feel what you feel.

And when that impression of your old self is clearer, and you detect the beginning of those feelings that you no longer need to allow, let your impression fade, let it shrink, let it recede into the distance. Watch it go, farther and farther away until it dissolves and disappears from view.

You don't need that version of your old self any more.

You have a new way to be. You are changing, because you've decided to change.

You have all the resources you need to make the changes you desire.

You have removed all obstacles to this change you want, by releasing the unwanted habits and beliefs, and leaving your old version behind, from this day forwards moving further from that state to a new more confident way of behaviour, more useful to you now and in the future.

Just allow that feeling of freedom and relief to filter through your whole body, wiping away the last remaining traces of that old way. Just let it go.

And now you can rest for a little while, and just allow yourself to drift deeper down.

Good.

Now, this is only one part of the story, so please continue to listen to the sound of my voice as you drift deeper down.

It is important that you now know that you have strengths or talents or abilities that not everyone possesses. You may or may not have skills that are rare or even unique, and these make you special.

And you are a kind and considerate person, although you may sometimes feel misunderstood or under-appreciated. It can be a hard struggle to keep up the pace of modern life, and you are quite right to sometimes think about your role in the world, and how you can best utilise your values, your skills, or your experience to benefit yourself and others.

When you feel good, it's infectious to those around you. When you have momentum, forward movement in your life, you get more as a bonus. And you know inside that you have more capacity to feel good and act positively, to express to the world your special, unique nature, and to observe each of theirs in return, because we're all unique and special in our own ways, and we're all looking to connect with other unique and special people.

And this tells you now, and the knowledge will stay with you from this day forwards, that although we are all different, we're also all the same. We are equal, even if it may not always be obvious how we are equal, but we're all made from the same stuff, and it is we ourselves who shape our relationship with the world and our place in it.

You alone decide for yourself, starting today by knowing and accepting that you are equal, and you are starting from the same place.

As you drift weightless and lazy in this place of learning, I'd like you to remember that you're equal, all the time, every day, so you now place your equality as the glowing centre of everything you learn and change, in your mind, fixed in place.

To make this happen, and you will make it happen easily, in your mind or out loud, it doesn't matter, using your best, most positive and confident internal voice, say along with me;

"I am equal. This is the truth."

"I am equal. This is the truth."

"I am equal. This is the truth."

Good.

And it is the truth, you are equal, and all and any hint that this was not always the case is now removed from the new version of you.

And at any time, in any place, from this day forward, should you ever face uncertainty about anything at all, you have this central belief deep in your body and your mind. Say it to yourself, or say it out-loud, say it often, and say it like you mean it:

"I am equal. This is the truth."

"I am equal. This is the truth."

"I am equal. This is the truth."

You are equal, and you own that truth. Nobody can diminish the truth that you are equal, no matter how hard they try, because your equality is your fundamental right as a human being, and you have always, and will always own it. You own that truth and you can defend that truth.

You are equal.

Good. Now just relax some more, and let your new version, the upgraded version of you, with its new freedom to explore, and equality, penetrate deep throughout your body and mind as you absorb the exciting possibilities of what may begin to happen for you, now you are making progress at an appropriate speed.

Take a moment to feel what you feel, and you may begin to notice a different sensation to what was there before, and you can know that even in this short time, change has begun.

<<Pause>>

And now you understand more where this feeling comes from, and you can agree with me that the simple way, to feel like this more often, is to know that you will feel this way each and every time you complete something, which you might not want to do.

And now you know how good it feels to succeed, even small, simple things, you might begin to wonder why you sometimes stepped back before today, and what it is that made you act that way.

But you need not wonder why any longer, because it really doesn't matter, just like many questions you may have had about before today, questions like why you felt or behaved in certain ways at certain times, but those things don't matter now, because the journey you have taken today, has enabled you to draw a line under the past, and from this day forwards there is a new version of yourself.

A real change has begun, a change that you decided to make and a change that will re-shape many aspects of your life, for the better, from this day forwards.

And your subconscious has clearly heard these messages, as you absorb and adopt them into your new version, your new habits and behaviours, and your subconscious has accepted this new information, as more appropriate and beneficial than the previous version, which has been deleted and is gone.

You may continue to imagine all the ways, in which your new behaviour will now benefit you, and those around you, or you may decide to switch off your thoughts, and just enjoy this time of peace and solitude. So just take a moment of quietness at your leisure, starting now...

<<Pause>>

Very good. Thank you for your focus and co-operation, you've been excellent in every way.

You've done great.

Emerge

PAUSE. In a moment I'm going to count from ONE up to THREE. At the count of three your eyes are going to open, become fully alert, totally refreshed. Any cobwebs that you might have had, any sleepiness of mind is going to dissolve and disappear, and you're going to feel bright eyed and full of energy.

You'll be fully alert and wonderful and marvellous in every way.

ONE, slowly easily and gently feel yourself coming back up to your full awareness,

At the count of TWO you're still relaxed and calm but notice that your eyes under your eyelids feel as if they're clearing, kind of like they're being bathed in a sparkling cool mountain stream, you feel GREAT.

On the next count those eyes are going to open, totally alert, fully refreshed, just feeling excited, wonderful, in every way, and every time you go into hypnosis you can let yourself go deeper than the time before because you know that just feels good.

All right, get ready, and on the count of THREE open those eyes and notice how good you feel.

Session 2 Transcript

So, once you've settled yourself, close your eyes, and let's start by taking the deep breath in, as usual, and this time, as you breathe out to start the journey, just allow yourself to smile a little, so that the descent into trance will be even more pleasurable than usual.

And breathe in – smile – breathe out, and feel a warm wave of relaxation spreading throughout your whole body, loosening and relaxing all the muscles around your joints, and just allowing yourself to push out any residual tension from those muscles and joints, just allowing yourself to go limp and floppy, lazy and relaxed, as you drift downwards into that calm, relaxed state where you have already demonstrated that you can make excellent and marvellous changes.

Now, you have often shown in the past that you are highly receptive to hypnosis, and that you can now go deeper and quicker into trance than the majority of people.

So you know that even now you are already much deeper than when you first started enjoying hypnosis because you have had so many interesting and remarkable experiences, and the things that you learned and discovered have already begun to benefit your life, so you can fully allow yourself to go deeper still, while you listen to the sound of my voice.

As you drift deeper down now, noticing the regularity of your breathing, and how the effect of breathing out each time leads you down deeper, more relaxed, and already you may be curious about what it is that you will learn this time, because every time you come here you learn new things, and every time your repeat those things you learn, they empower and support you more each day,

And you might wonder if there is any limit to the things you can learn or the habits you can change when you are in this relaxed, deep, comfortable, safe space, and I can tell you that there are no limits, because no-one has discovered the limits, as no-one has found any limit to how deeply relaxed you can become, so you can always go deeper, and you will go deeper now, so go on – let yourself go deeper now.

That's good, you're now so deep that you know that your body is completely relaxed, and your mind is open and ready to receive new learning, that you can add new resources that will strengthen you.

And I want you to know that everything we're going to do today is scientific. Everything we do today will use the power of knowledge to affect the parts of you, the parts of your body itself, that determine how you respond, in every situation. And you already learned how to do this, and now you're going to learn how to make yourself more powerful, stronger, and more resilient.

Now, as you drift gently downwards into a deeper state of relaxation, conscious only of the gently rhythm of your breathing and the sound of my voice, I have some more useful information that you might like to know.

The Work

Now you have shown in the past that you are highly receptive to hypnosis, and that you can now go deeper and quicker into trance than the majority of people.

So you know that even now you are already much deeper than when you first started enjoying hypnosis because you have had so many interesting and remarkable experiences whilst in trance, and the things that you learned and discovered have already begun to benefit your life, so you can fully allow yourself to go deeper still, while you listen to the sound of my voice.

And you may wonder why everyone in the world would like to try this, to be so wonderfully, beautifully relaxed in every way, and those other people have not yet realised how good this can be, and in the future many more people will be able to know that going into this relaxed, uncomplicated state opens up parts of your mind that can enable genuine, useful, simple changes for a better, more fulfilling life. This is knowledge you possess.

So, as you drift deeper down, noticing the regularity of your breathing, and how the effect of breathing out each time leads you down deeper, more relaxed, and already you may be curious about what it is that you will learn this time, because every time you come here you learn new things, and every time your repeat those things you learn, they empower and support you more each day,

and you might wonder if there is any limit to the things you can learn or the habits you can change when you are in this relaxed, deep, comfortable, safe space,

And I can tell you that there are no limits, because no-one has discovered the limits, as no-one has found any limit to how deeply relaxed you can become, so you can always go deeper, and you will go deeper now, so go on – let yourself go deeper now.

That's good, you're now so deep that you know that your body is completely relaxed, and your mind is open and ready to receive new learning, that you can add new resources that will strengthen you and enable you to always be the calm, confident person that people look towards whenever calmness and confidence are the best ways to behave in any situation.

And you may find, and I hope you find, that you're here in your basement of relaxation, because each and every time that you come to your basement of relaxation you know that good things happen, useful skills are learned, and you add to the pleasure and positivity of your life, because it is your human right to be happy and content. And you are here today to claim all your human rights, to equality and confidence.

Now that you're relaxed here in your basement of relaxation, I'd like once again to remind you of how proud I am of the commitment you have continued to make, and that you have discovered for yourself how listening to the sound of my voice, and following the instructions you are given, helps to empower you, from this day forwards.

Now that you are armed with the reassuring proof of your abilities, you are enabled to go to another level of understanding and control, to use your body itself, and to be in command of the way your body responds to difficult or challenging situations, which don't really bother you so much any more because you already learned how to manage them.

There is only forward momentum, to make progress, and then to complete their task and enjoy the rewarding and satisfying feeling that comes from successfully accomplishing something challenging.

I'd like you to use your powerful imagination to go deep inside and find a situation when you did not feel as confident as you would have liked to feel, and go inside to access the way you were before the event or situation. Even if you cannot access a specific memory, and that's fine too, you can clearly imagine the scenario I'm sure, so do that now, and I'll give you a moment of silence whilst you do that now.

<<Pause>>

Found it? Good. Now focus all your attention on that feeling, and see how it grows, and maybe takes on a shape or a colour.

<<Pause>>

And now maybe you can feel it rising, like a kind of anxiety, and you're already searching for your old familiar safety mechanism to get away from the feeling, to back off from the challenge.

And as this feeling you have found came by your command, so we can make it go away, also by your command.

I'd like you now to focus on your breathing. Just be a spectator, you don't have to do anything. All this time you've been in this deeply relaxed state, your breathing has been happening slowly and gently in the background, nourishing and supporting your body as you rest.

Now, in a moment, you're going to deepen your breathing. When you're ready, you're going to breathe in much deeper, and as you exhale that breath, long and slow, you'll be aware that the feeling you had before starts to dissipate and diminish, so try that now, and on the next breath, inhale deeply.... And *exhale slowly, that's right, and feel the calmness returning to your body, that's right.*

Take a few breaths this way....

All that momentary tension has slipped away, and you can be certain that in each instance that may happen when you feel the anxiety rising, and if you ever notice the urge to retreat, you can breathe deeply whilst you collect your thoughts, and the calmness will return and you'll be ready for anything.

And when you breathe deeper, you will naturally stand taller, and you may have noticed that the calm, confident people you meet often look like they're posture is very upright. Confident people use all their attributes positively, and standing tall not only communicates confidence to others, but makes you feel more confident yourself.

Now that you've learned how to return yourself to normal when a confident performance is required, perhaps you'd like to learn how to feel better than normal in the same situation. Because when you feel good, you look good, and you perform well.

Here I will remind you that you also know that there is wisdom in the world, but whether you choose to accept things that you hear and are told often depends on whether you believe that the person telling you has acquired real knowledge, or is simply repeating things they have heard themselves.

A good example of this is when other people may tell you to smile, when you are short of confidence, or having a difficult time. And in the past you may have disregarded this casual advice as just something that people say because they don't have anything else to offer you.

And in fact that is true, everyone says you should smile, but no-one really explains why it should be true, because it is, scientifically true.

When you smile, a big broad smile which moves your whole face, the action of the tiny muscles at the side of your head stimulates part of your brain, to release those same reward chemicals we explored earlier.

And you may be quite interested to hear that this happens even when you make your smile for no reason. You simply make yourself smile, and the effects will happen.

So, when you're ready, tell yourself to smile, the biggest, brightest smile you can manage, and hold it, push it wider, make that smile even bigger...

And feel that positive reward sensation start to move down from your head through your upper body, and you can make it last as long as you like, but that's probably enough for now, you have experienced the positive chemical and mood-altering effects of a smile, even a forced smile, and you can add this knowledge to the secrets you have now learned from the calm, confident people that you are now becoming.

And you can know that the smile you make will send a powerful message of confidence and self-esteem whenever you show it to others.

And from this day forwards, should you at any time feel that old anxiety deep down, you will know it is in your complete control to crush it, with the simple, easy, effective secrets you have learned here today.

Breathe and Smile

Breathe and Smile

Breathe and Smile

And from this day forwards you will always show your confident self to others, and you will disallow old beliefs or apprehensions to intrude into your thoughts, because you are moving forwards, making progress, and leaving behind any false or redundant restrictions.

Nothing now holds you back; you start each day equal to everyone, and you climb upwards from that point.

You prepare well for every situation. You have interesting things to say, and you know the right time to say them.

You have new skills and new ways to calm yourself, and these are now automatic habits that you will use without thinking.

You focus on the outcome, always looking forwards, and the satisfaction and good feelings that will always accompany every achievement.

And you now know that you have all the resources you need, and all the skills to use them appropriately.

And soon you'll be returning to your life, and you can be proud that this time, you bring with you new attributes, new abilities, and the certainty and clarity that you have made the change you decided to make, and which will now serve you well through your whole life.

Emerge

Now, you may be in a beautiful relaxed state right now, and you may want to stay here, and maybe slip off to sleep in a few moments. If that is your desire, that's fine, so you can relax even more now and you don't need to pay attention to anything else I say.

If you would prefer to emerge yourself, you already know how to do this, by slowly counting from one to three, and progressively clearing your mind before opening your eyes on count of three, so please feel free to do that for yourself right now.

∼

Session 3 Transcript

So, first check yourself to make sure you're absolutely ready to go into trance, and when you know it's time, take a slow, deep breath in, hold it for a second, close your eyes, and release it at your own speed.

As the breath flows out of you, feel your body begin to anticipate how good it's going to feel to let yourself relax deeply as you've done before, and let your body relax, whilst you allow your breathing to find it's own, slow, steady rhythm, breathing in – and out – at exactly the correct speed for your body to take the nourishment it needs from each and every breath, and on your next breath in, I'd like to you to now open your eyes at the top of the breath, and then as you release the breath from your body, allow your eyes to close gently again. Good.

And now, as you breathe at your own speed, you feel your whole body begin to synchronise with your breathing, so that each time you breathe in you feel the life-giving air flowing through your whole body, and as you breathe out each time, you allow yourself to become even more deeply relaxed, feeling lazy and wonderful, and you know how good it will feel to go deeper so why not allow yourself to go all the way down now, as I start to count from ten down to one.

Ten – You are committed to finding a state of deep relaxation this time and every time you use hypnosis, and just this thought may be enough that you already begin to feel yourself more relaxed than a few moments before.

Nine – And so you have given yourself permission to do nothing else right now than allow the lazy, sensual feeling of releasing all the tension from your muscles and joints as you begin to settle into the journey to calmness and tranquility

Eight – Deeper still, your body now so limp and floppy that you start to lose touch with your physical awareness, as you place your body in temporary hibernation – you won't be needing it for a little while, so allow it to rest

Seven – Move your attention to your face, and as you become aware of how your skin and tiny muscles of your face can easily be made to relax even more, and your face feels different now, and it's a wonderful, careless, lazy feeling as you completely release those muscles and just allow yourself to be

Six – Now your body and your face are totally relaxed and drifting safely, I'd like you to turn your attention back to your breathing and you can notice how this state of deep relaxation has slowed your breathing even more, and

Five – each time you breathe out, you naturally go deeper, as you've done before, and you possess knowledge about how effortlessly you can settle into this deepened state of consciousness, where you are the beneficiary of the personal power of change, and

Four – Now you begin to notice that your breathing is happening deeper in your body, lower down in your abdomen, and that kind of breathing feels good to you, and it is good, the best kind of breathing

Three – And now your body is at rest, and your breathing is happening at exactly the right speed, as you slowly drift down to that relaxed state that you've enjoyed so much so many times, and you know how good it feels

Two – As you start to notice that your descent is slowing as you reach the basement of your relaxation, and you may be curious about what will be the positive effect this time, and

One- You're there, totally relaxed, feeling wonderful, and you may now rest for a moment and settle into the gentle rhythm, aware of your regular, slow, controlled breathing, and allowing it to happen and your whole self to synchronise, and take a moment of silence to appreciate how you are right now...

<<Pause>>

Good, that's right.

Now that you have once more achieved this state of deep relaxation, listening only to the sound of my voice, and relaxing in *rhythm with your breathing, you may begin to feel curious about what you will learn this time.*

Before we get onto that, you have the opportunity to reflect on the progress you've made, and how that makes you feel. You've travelled a long way from where you started.

The mental discipline that you're learning here may be one of the most useful things you'll add to your life.

Allow yourself to begin to feel, somewhere deep inside, a tiny glow of satisfaction, because you're now thinking and acting differently. You have understood and allowed yourself the capacity to make important changes, changes that will improve your happiness, your confidence, and your life.

The Work

Now, we're going to use your powerful imagination again, to bring up an image or impression that we can use together, to develop certain knowledge and abilities that you now have.

You proved that you have the resources. You proved that you understand how to combine them. And you proved how you can generate positive, rewarding feelings of confidence and accomplishment when you use the skills you've learned and the resources you have in an appropriate way.

I'd like you to more deeply relax now, and allow your mind to go into a peaceful, restful state, however that comes to you.

And in this restful state you may find yourself temporarily alone, in a calm, warm, hospitable place. It's dark in this place, which you're enjoying, and you can be sure that you're alone, and no-one else is there. Take a moment to get used to the dimness.

And as you allow yourself to become increasingly calm and at home in this dark place, more calm and comfortable in yourself than before, you may begin to notice a soft circular glow on the floor in front of you, and you can see that the glow on the floor is coming from a single spotlight, far above your head.

Now this spotlight is a special one, very personal to you, and you can control its brightness and intensity, and its colour and movement, simply with your mind. If you want the beam to change, so that the circle of light in front of you changes, you can make that happen.

So let's try that now.

Look at the circle of light on the floor, and concentrate on making it brighter, at your own speed. That's good, just allow that beam to brighten as you control it with your mind.

Now, when you've made it bright enough, gradually begin to reduce the brightness, and allow the circle of light to grow dimmer, a little at a time, that's good.

Now that you have complete control of this spotlight beam, I can tell you that there are more things you can do to control it, with your mind.

First of all, just like you did before, adjust the brightness of the beam so that you're most comfortable with it. The perfect blend of light and dark. So now, maintaining that circle as it is now, go inside yourself, as quickly as you can allow yourself, and find a time when you felt happy and confident, and able to achieve anything, and let me give you a few seconds to find that feeling and maybe where it's located in your body.

<<Pause>>

Good, you've found something. Well done. Now, we don't need to know about whatever made you feel this way, so you can place all your attention on the feeling itself, and you know that when you have good feelings in your body that you can amplify and magnify them so that they feel even better, and maybe you will do this by imagining the colour of the feeling, and a strong colour often indicates a strong feeling, and if you make the colour stronger and brighter, the feeling will grow stronger and brighter too. And maybe you can cause the feeling to move, maybe in a ball or a loop, and it can physically grow from the place in your body where you first found it, and you can make it bigger, and let it rotate or spin or vibrate through your whole body, and you may be quite surprised at how you are able to do this, because the more you practice, the stronger and brighter you can make that feeling, and you know that this is the correct feeling for confidence, and an appropriate feeling to use now.

Now you can preserve this feeling, the confident way that you feel right now, by placing the shape or colour of this satisfying, fulfilling feeling into the circle of light on the floor in front of you. You send the feeling into the spotlight that you control, do it now, and before your eyes that feeling from your body is now in front of you, bright and vibrant, and awaiting your instruction.

In a moment, on my count of three, you'll be stepping into the spotlight, and when you do, you'll understand that this spotlight is under your control and you have programmed it to beam the best and most confident part of you, that immense feeling you generated, so that you can step into the spotlight and be that confident, competent person that delivers the right messages, in the right way, that everyone clearly understands and you will always have the resources you need and a clear path ahead of you.

Get ready, one – two – three, and step forward into the beam, and let the light wash over you, flooding you with that feeling you experienced before, the sum of all your parts, the combination of all your personal resources, and the clear, ordered mental approach to any task.

And once again, let the feeling grow and move and brighten inside and you're beginning to notice that everything about you is now different, and you feel disconnected from the old you; it's hard to recall how you may have felt in the past, it's just a distant memory like maybe you read about it in a magazine or heard it on the radio;

You're different now.

You decided to change, and you made the change happen

You can move forwards now, only forwards.

In this beam of light, you can be whoever you need to be, for as long as you need, because you have all the resources to get the job done. And you may say to yourself, anytime you're preparing,

"I have all the resources I need to get the job done"

"I have all the resources I need to get the job done"

"I have all the resources I need to get the job done"

Good, now...

Allow yourself to feel deeply satisfied that you've understood this so completely, and now just allow yourself to step out of the light for a moment, and reduce its brightness to save resources for a while, until you need it again.

Still remaining deeply relaxed and comfortable in this darkened place with the dim spotlight projecting your confidence before you, you remain completely unchanged and totally calm as you begin to notice a few people appearing like a small audience in the darkness.

You are absolutely, completely relaxed and comfortable that these people, who you may know, or who may be strangers, are coming to hear you speak, because you know your subject, and you always take time to prepare well.

The people in your audience are here willingly, and hoping that you will teach or inform them about something that they will benefit from, and which you know all about.

These people in this audience are here to receive a transfer of knowledge or information from your mind to theirs, and their wish and desire is to feel comfortable and calm whilst receiving the knowledge from you, because that's the way that knowledge is best shared between people.

And now the audience is complete. They are quiet and ready for you, yes, because it's you that they've come here to see tonight, doing what you do. And you know how this works, because you've been preparing for this for a little while now, and you've got all the tools and secret weapons you can now use, smoothly and automatically, to project the, calm, confident version of you.

Please follow my instructions as I count from one to three...

One: For a moment, just focus on your posture, and check you're physically ready, that you can stand tall so that you project confidence and authority, so check your posture now and make sure you're ready.

The spotlight beam in front of you is starting to brighten a little, and on

Two: Briefly shift your attention to your content or material; it doesn't matter what it is today, you know it intimately. You can rely on yourself for that, because you allowed enough time to properly learn and understand your subject and rehearse the messages you are going to deliver to your audience, and the beam in front of you now is brighter still, and on...

Three, you're completely ready, you squeeze your hands together, as you feel a little rush of anticipation and confidence about what you're about to do,

And STEP FORWARDS into the beam, and let that light wash over you and the strong and growing feeling of confidence and self-assurance, growing brighter and more colourful as you absorb it through your whole body, and that feeling of mastery and confidence takes you over, and you drift for a moment just to feel how good this feels, and congratulating yourself that you can have this feeling of confidence and self-assurance any time you need it, because you know how to make it happen, and you're making it happen right now.

Good, well done.

And you know that things are different now, better, brighter and more in focus, and the old, anxious, nervous you has no part to play from today forwards, and you always had all the resources you needed to feel stronger and more capable, and now you've learned how to use those resources, those excellent parts of you that bring energy and knowledge to everything that you're going to do from now on, because when you share your energy and knowledge about your chosen subject with others, you enrich their lives with more energy and knowledge, and that knowledge brings value to everyone you meet.

And any time you are given the opportunity to present or speak in the future;

you have new tools; you know your subject and you rehearse so that you are completely confident in what you have to say;

You bring your positive energies together simply by squeezing them together in your hands;

And you have your own personal spotlight, that you control, that will always ensure that your best energy and confidence is available for you to use, because you make it happen, whenever you step into the light.

And now you have these tools at your disposal, you practice them often and you look forward to the next time you are invited to share knowledge with others, because you have mastered your art and you are set up to succeed every time you do this.

Now let this knowledge, and your new confidence, filter through your mind and find its permanent place, deep inside, where it will automatically replace old, unwanted habits that held you back before.

Take a few quiet moments to let that happen, starting now...

Pause

Well done.

Now in a moment I'm going to gently emerge you. You'll remember everything you've done and every place you've been....

EMERGE

In a moment I'm going to count from ONE up to THREE. At the count of three your eyes are going to open, become fully alert, totally refreshed. Any cobwebs that you might have had, any sleepiness of mind is going to dissolve and disappear, and you're going to feel bright eyed and full of energy.

You'll be fully alert and wonderful and marvellous in every way. ONE, slowly easily and gently feel yourself coming back up to your full awareness,

At the count of TWO you're still relaxed and calm but notice that your eyes under your eyelids feel as if they're clearing, kind of like they're being bathed in a sparkling cool mountain stream, you feel GREAT.

On the next count those eyes are going to open, totally alert, fully refreshed, just feeling excited, wonderful, in every way, and every time you go into hypnosis you can let yourself go deeper than the time before because you know that just feels good.

All right, get ready, and on the count of THREE open those eyes and notice how good you feel.

17

PROGRAM DEBRIEF

CONGRATULATIONS! You've now completed the *Cool, Calm, Confident You* program.

If you've been taking this course to improve your business presentation confidence, don't stop here. Repeat the recording as often as you can, and it will magnify the effects. Once you can switch this stuff on and off at will, which won't take you long, you'll find you've acquired one of the most important career advancement tools there is.

If your interest is less business and more social, perhaps a wedding speech or something like that, get in as much practice with the recording and your material as you can. Being confident means you must be ready.

The more you practice, the more readily you'll be able to

spin up the good feelings that go with your new confidence. Taking that kind of armour into any presentation or speaking situation will automatically transmit your knowledge and enthusiasm to your audience, whether it's one person at an interview or ten thousand in a conference centre. In the public speaking world, it's the confident performers who get the best gigs.

I wish you luck and good fortune in whatever you choose to do with it.

OTHER RICK SMITH PROGRAMS & BOOKS

IF YOU'VE ENJOYED *Cool, Calm, Confident You,* here are some other programs which might interest you:

∼

Stress - Take Control and Crush It, Now.

You know what it's like. That old familiar feeling starts to trouble you; it grows and mutates, sucking your energy, attention, and logical thought into a ball of aching tension, clouding your judgment and influencing your actions.

It starts in your head, but it invades your whole body, and you hate it.

Time for action...

You're Not Alone - You Can Fix Yourself

Chronic or ongoing stress can wreak havoc on your body, significantly raising your risk of serious illness. Scientists now consider underlying stress to be one of the top-three hidden killers.

The main culprit is *cortisol*, a naturally occurring, usually benign steroid hormone, which regulates many of your body's important functions. But when uncontrolled cortisol is allowed to flood your body, the damage is serious, and cumulative.

Once you understand what's happening, it's not that difficult to adapt your response so that the cortisol effects are suppressed, and you remain stable and grounded without losing your focus.

Using hypnosis, you'll learn to equalise before cortisol scores: simple techniques and routines that will enable you to remain cool and calm in the face of your challenges and navigate yourself - and those around you - through those difficult times.

By the time you complete the three sessions, repeating them as necessary, you'll have acquired all the tools and techniques you need to face any situation with calmness, and confidence in your ability to deal with any challenge.

And you'll feel a whole lot better than you do right now!

Explore 'Crush Stress Now' at ricksmithhypnosis.com

So, What's Holding You Back?

Whatever happened to your easy life? These days, there's so much to do. It saps your energy and your focus. Some days you just can't be bothered...

Need A Little Help to Get Moving?

Your *logical* brain knows what you need to do, and when and how to do it. But your *emotional* brain is pulling you backwards, acting like a hacker, sending you false code -

- *"Don't start that task because we might fail, and we know how that feels!"*

- *"It's so cosy here on the sofa, we can paint the fence some other time!"*

- *"We don't need a promotion, who wants to hustle that hard?"*

So you languish in your comfort zone, fooling yourself that this is the life you want, when you're actually feeling guilty, embarrassed, or ashamed because you know it's not the life you really need.

When you're demotivated like this, life can be pretty joyless.

You can be better.

Here Comes the Fix...

Your situation is your emotional *bad code,* causing you to behave sub-optimally, and it's holding you back from achieving your potential.

In the three sessions of *The Motivation Code,* we'll hunt down that broken code, and replace it with new, effective code that will fire your positive, energetic "Let's Get This Done" response instead of your old "Let's Not Bother Today" submission.

Explore 'The Motivation Code'

CRUSH ANXIETY NOW
HYPNOSIS MEETS SCIENCE
3-HOUR HYPNOTHERAPY AUDIO PROGRAM
hypnosis.com

Anxiety - you feel it rising, so take control and crush it, now.

You know what it's like. That old familiar feeling starts to trouble you; it grows and mutates, sucking your energy, attention, and logical thought into a ball of aching tension, clouding your judgment and influencing your actions. You hate it, and it never helps. Whatever you've tried hasn't worked, so you're looking for something different.

You're not alone - you can fix yourself

Anxiety comes in many forms, but it's usually caused by fear of something that you think is about to happen, and the way that it's going to make you feel. Your imagination perceives an impending threat and fires off a salvo of chemicals into your brain and bloodstream to alert you. Many people suffer all their lives, and never acknowledge that they need help to get on top of the condition.

Yet, once you understand what's happening, it's not that difficult to adapt your response so that the effects of these chemicals are suppressed, and you get back to normal quickly without losing your focus. Using hypnosis, you'll learn to separate your thoughts and feelings when anxiety approaches, and to focus on the outcome, not the process. You'll be able to remain cool and calm in the face of your challenges, and navigate yourself, and those around you, through those difficult situations.

By the time you complete the three sessions, repeating them as necessary, you'll have acquired all the tools and techniques you need to face any situation with calmness, and confidence in your ability to deal with any challenge.

And you'll feel a whole lot better than you do right now!

Explore 'Crush Anxiety Now'

Why Are You Still Putting Things Off?

Procrastination - You hate it, and it never helps. How come other people seem to get things done? You know what it's like. You've things to do but you're finding every possible reason to avoid getting started.

Why does it always have to be this way?

You're Not Alone

Many people suffer all their lives, and never acknowledge that they need help to get on top of the bad habits and anxiety that comes with putting things off.

- Maybe you're a perfectionist? You don't want to start something because you're fearful of your ability to complete it to your own high standards, even though you may have done it – successfully - many times before.

- Or perhaps you feel inadequate or unworthy? You think – usually wrongly – that you're going to fail, so you'd rather not take the risk. Even though you know this is an illogical mind-set.

- Or is it simply that you hate the things you have to do, so you find any reason to avoid doing them? Until you absolutely have to!

You feel trapped, a hostage to procrastination.

It Doesn't Have To Be This Way

In these hypnosis sessions, we'll approach the challenge from all sides. Each recording is progressive: you'll learn and practice something and then carry that skill forwards to the next session.

By the time you complete the three sessions, you'll have

mastered the capability to remain fully focused and highly motivated in every situation, knowing full well that the rewards of powering ahead are many times greater than those of holding back.

Explore 'Do It Now - Crush Procrastination'

∽

ricksmithhypnosis.com

AFTERWORD

The Scripts Used in this Book

The recordings we used in this program can be streamed or downloaded free once you register at

http://tiny.cc/amzconf

If you encounter any issues obtaining the recordings, please e-mail me and I'll fix it for you.

rick@ricksmithhypnosis.com

If you enjoy the book and you find something worthwhile in the system, please take a moment to post a Review on Amazon.

However you decide to use your new skills, above all - *enjoy the journey!*

Rick Smith